GETTING INTO........

BLUEGRASS BANJO

by ALAN MUNDE

Online Audio   www.melbay.com/20803BCDEB

2 3 4 5 6 7 8 9 0

Visit us on the Web at www.melbay.com — E-mail us at email@melbay.com

Getting Into Bluegrass Banjo
By Alan Munde

Contents

SECTION 1: Getting Started

Introduction

This course is designed for anyone interested in a well-founded, straightforward introduction to the essentials of bluegrass-style banjo. Whether you have never played a stringed instrument, are learning the banjo as a second instrument, or have struggled with other methods, this course will be of great help. It covers just that information needed to get the basic movements of the style together.

The ideas and approaches I offer in this text were developed from my many years of teaching bluegrass at South Plains College in Levelland, Texas, and my even greater number of years as a professional touring and recording artist. This text has been used by other instructors and their students with good results.

A well-rounded musician needs many other techniques and bits of musical knowledge that are not covered in this text. Please consult with private instructors and other instruction material, watch and listen to all the music you can, and talk to players about the many aspects of playing music. You will need every scrap of information you can get to be the best player you can possibly be.

I hope you enjoy your time learning, and then performing, in the bluegrass banjo style.

Hints and Suggestions

Before you begin, let me offer some ideas on music and practice. In my approach to music instruction, there are four basic areas of study. Although they are presented separately, they are interdependent and interactive.

1. Ear Training and Music Theory. Just as you are trained from youth to use language, you will need to develop your ear to hear music and recognize its patterns, rhythms, and tonal textures. In bluegrass banjo you will want to begin listening for melodies, rhythms, chord changes, roll patterns, fingering techniques and song forms. Music theory may sound scary, but it is the result of hundreds of years of very smart people listening to and making observations about music. Some of their observations are connected to physics, others to culture and taste. In this presentation I cover very little music theory, so again, you may need to search out the information and ask many questions. In bluegrass, the theory is very straightforward and understandable. As you learn more about the normal occurrences in music as expressed in music theory, the more you can hear and apply those concepts to your playing and add interesting and beautiful ideas to your arrangements.

2. Technique. This area is about how to hold your hands and fingers, and how to move them gracefully and efficiently through the motions needed to play. Consult with local players and/or instructors for developing the details of your hand position.

3. Practice. After you feel you have the proper technique, you will need to repeat the motions many times to cement them into your mind and muscles. It takes many repetitions of these micro-muscular movements to play properly and to ingrain them so that they become gestures. Practice each new roll, left-hand technique, or new tune enough that when you pick up your banjo, those new things are in your fingers as readily as words are in your mouth.

4. Style. This is where you put Ear Training, Technique, and Practice together into a way of playing the bluegrass banjo. In this area you should learn the traditional literature of the music and standards such as " Roll In My Sweet Baby's Arms," " Foggy Mountain Breakdown," " Old Joe Clark," and hundreds of other tunes that are part of bluegrass music. In addition, you should work toward creating new arrangements in the style. The ability to do this comes from a great deal of listening, a deep understanding of the music, and an understanding of its roots and boundaries.

Remember that study in one area will generate new study in one or all of the other areas.

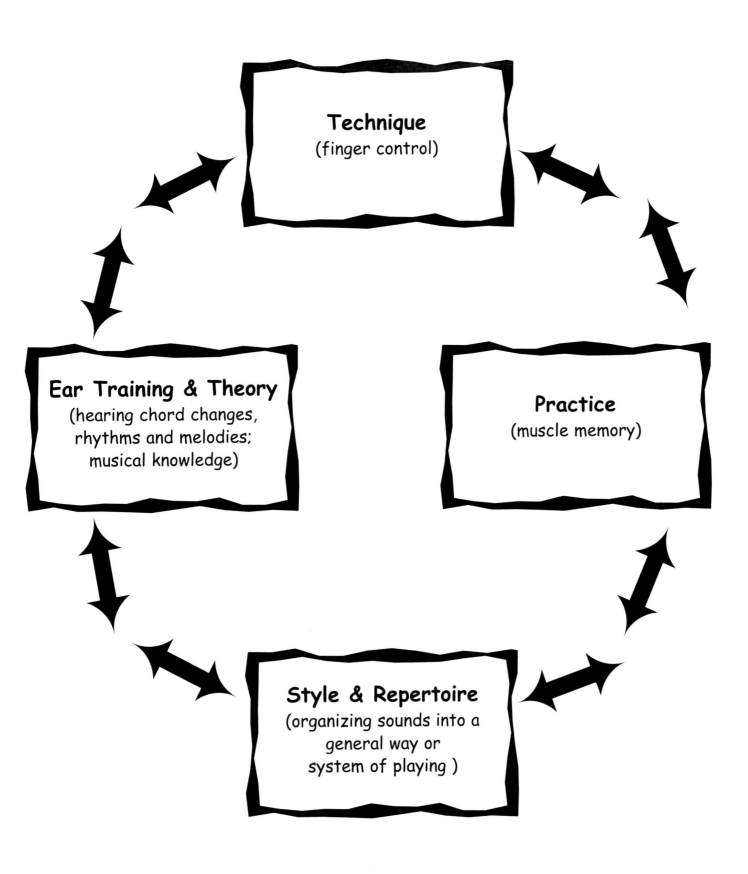

Technique
(finger control)

Ear Training & Theory
(hearing chord changes,
rhythms and melodies;
musical knowledge)

Practice
(muscle memory)

Style & Repertoire
(organizing sounds into a
general way or
system of playing)

A Few Hints on Practice

There is no one best practice regimen. You will need to discover what works best for you. I can suggest some things that may be helpful:

- Compare your playing with that of bluegrass banjo players on recordings.

- Play along with recorded playing if possible. Even if you can keep up for only a few measures, do it.

- Dampen the strings with your left-hand, and play familiar rolls in time with recorded music to get the picking hand into the rhythmical feel and flow of the music.

- Play for other players and ask for advice.

- Record or videotape yourself and watch or listen.

- Watch admired players and try to imitate the grace, efficiency, and smoothness of their hands as they play.

- Watch your hands in a mirror as you play and try to imitate admired players.

- Seek advice and critiques of your playing.

- Play along with a metronome, drum machine, or other rhythm-keeping device.

- Check the tablature to ensure that you are performing the exercise or piece accurately.

- Be successful with very small bites of material and then build on those small successes.

The Banjo and its Parts

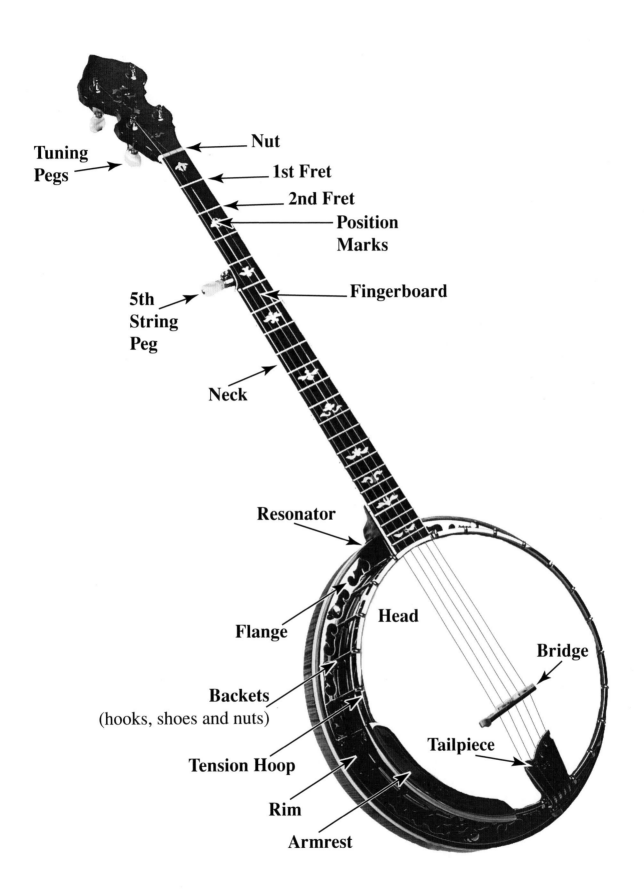

Tuning Pegs

Nut

1st Fret

2nd Fret

Position Marks

Fingerboard

5th String Peg

Neck

Resonator

Flange

Head

Bridge

Backets (hooks, shoes and nuts)

Tension Hoop

Tailpiece

Rim

Armrest

Parts of the Banjo

It is helpful to be familiar with the parts of the modern bluegrass-style banjo and to have some idea of their function.

The **NECK** is the whole of the slim portion of the banjo that the strings run along, including the headstock, fingerboard, and heel.

The **HEADSTOCK** is the area of the neck where the strings are attached. Notice that it is angled back so as to apply tension on the strings as they press down over the nut. It is also the area displaying the banjo maker's name.

The **TUNING PEGS** are the mechanical devices the strings attach to, that allow the tension of the strings to be changed for tuning the instrument. Notice that the fifth-string peg is located at the fifth fret on the top side of the neck.

The **NUT** is the small notched piece that separates the headstock from the fingerboard and stops the vibration of the unfretted strings.

The **FINGERBOARD** is the part of the banjo on which the fingers press the strings in order to shorten or lengthen them.

The **FRETS** are the metal bands running across and dividing the banjo neck into steps (two frets) and half-steps (one fret). The spaces between the fret wires are also referred to as frets.

For example, the space between the nut and the first metal wire is the first fret; the space between the first metal wire and the second metal wire is the second fret, and so on. They will be used to identify where to place your fingers. For example, "place your first finger on the first fret of the second string." When you place your finger, do not press on top of the fret wire but just behind it. You are actually pressing the string down onto the metal wire, which causes the string to stop vibrating at the point where it contacts the fret wire.

The **BRIDGE** is the part of the banjo that transfers the vibration of the strings to the head. It is at the opposite end of the string from the nut, and stops the vibration of the string. The string, when played open, vibrates between the nut and the bridge. Notice that the strings arch over the bridge and that there is some tension which holds the bridge in place. The bridge can move as the tension is decreased, as when you are changing the strings. Its placement is important for the proper intonation of the instrument.

The **TAILPIECE** is the part of the banjo that the strings attach to, at the opposite end from the headstock.

The **ARMREST** is for the comfort of your arm as it lies on the banjo in the normal playing position.

The **HEAD** is the large vibrating membrane that transfers the vibrations to the rest of the banjo and to the air inside and outside the instrument. Its tension can be adjusted and affects the overall sound of the instrument. The head is replaceable and comes in several varieties and sizes.

The **TENSION HOOP** is the metal hoop that presses down on the head. It exerts firm, uniform pressure on the head and holds it in place at tension.

The **BRACKETS** are the metal pieces with curved ends that hook into the slots in the tension hoop and pass through the flange. They are tightened with nuts on the opposite side of the flange and are adjusted to tighten or loosen the head tension.

The **FLANGE** is the metal plate that fits around the perimeter of the banjo and holds the brackets as they leverage pressure against the tension hoop.

The **RESONATOR** is the wooden back of the banjo and forms the resonating cavity. It colors and projects the sound of the banjo.

The **RIM** is the round wooden frame that the parts rest against or are attached to.

The **TONE RING** is the metal ring that fits on top of the rim underneath the head. It is the heaviest part of the bluegrass-style banjo, and possibly the most important element in the banjo sound.

The **COORDINATING RODS** are the metal rods inside the banjo. Most banjos have two coordinating rods. They have a two-fold function. First, they are threaded on the inside and attach to the lug bolts in the heel of the neck that pass through the rim. They tighten to hold the neck firmly to the rim. Second, they are used in a crude fashion to adjust the string action (the height of the strings above the neck, usually expressed as the distance from the strings to the top of the twelfth fret). This is an adjustment that should be made by person experienced in set-up.

The **TENSION ROD** is a threaded rod located under the fingerboard. It protrudes into the headstock and has a fitting that can be turned with a socket driver for adjustment. It controls the necessary bow in the neck and should be adjusted by person experienced in set-up. The adjustable end is usually covered by a tension rod cover.

The **SET-UP** is the combination of proper fits, adjustments and parts that make up the sound of the banjo. Much importance is given by master players to set-up. Set-up is like fine tuning a machine and requires some years of experience and practice. Find a banjo-playing friend or a repair person you feel confident with to help you through the many interrelated adjustments that can affect the sound of your banjo. In time you will have a pretty good understanding of the process.

Speed

A common way to increase speed is to find a comfortable metronome setting. Practice at that speed until you are able to play correctly and completely. Then move the metronome setting up a few beats per minute and try again. As you are successful at each new setting, keep moving up until you run into difficulties. Keep challenging yourself until you reach a tempo that is close to or beyond a performance tempo.

Here is another approach. Take a short complete phrase that you have rehearsed and are comfortable with. Relax and play it as fast as you can without regard to a metronome setting – throw yourself into it without worrying about mistakes. This will give your fingers experience with moving quickly. Make playing faster a part of each practice session no matter where you are in the course.

Reading Banjo Tablature

- Each staff line represents one string of the banjo. (The first string is closest to the floor when you are playing the banjo.)

- Numbers indicating the fret to be fingered by the left-hand will appear on the line. For example:

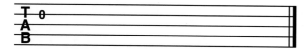

This indicates that you should finger the third string at the third fret.

A zero represents an open string. Here it shows an open second string:

- The staff will be divided into measures by *bar* lines:

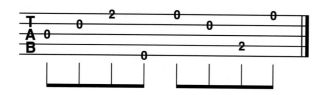

In most cases, a measure will contain the equivalent of eight eighth notes. Here are two groups of four eighth notes.

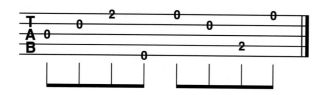

- Numbers above the staff indicate left-hand fingering; letters below the staff indicate right-hand fingering.

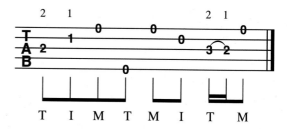

- Eighth notes get one-half a beat each.

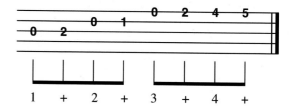

- You will also see quarter notes, which are indicated by a single descending stem. These last *twice* as long as eighth notes, or 1 beat.

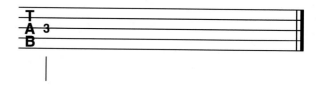

In addition, there are sixteenth notes which are played twice as fast as eighth notes and are indicated by a double beam.

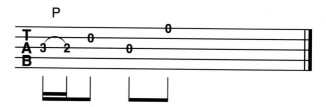

Use a pull-off for these quick notes if the numbers are going lower, and a hammer-on or slide if the numbers are going higher.

Here is an example of a measure that includes sixteenth, eighth and quarter notes:

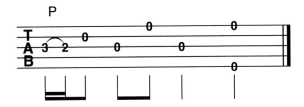

A half note, or two beats, is indicated by a number without a stem.

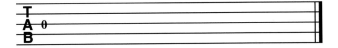

A whole note, or four beats, is indicated by two numbers with a tie.

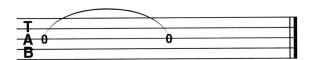

Three beats are indicted by a dotted half note.

The Capo

Many players use a piece of equipment called a capo (pronounced "kay-po"). It allows us to play in keys other than G and still use all the licks and positions we have learned. The capo is a clamp device that fits around the neck and holds down the first, second, third, and fourth strings to create a sort of moveable nut. The fifth string will also have to be capoed at the same number of frets as the regular capo – i.e. if the capo is placed at the second fret, the fifth string will need to be capoed at the seventh. Thus you have a banjo capo and a fifth string capo (some people use a number of small miniature railroad spikes under the fifth string. The string is slipped under the spike and it frets the string). With this in place, we can play just as if we were in the key of G, but it will sound in the new key without any changes in the playing.

Capo placement	The key you think you are playing in	The key that is sounded
2nd fret	G	A
3rd fret	G	B♭
4th fret	G	B
5th fret	G	C

Tuning the Five-String Banjo

If you have access to a piano you may tune your banjo as shown below.

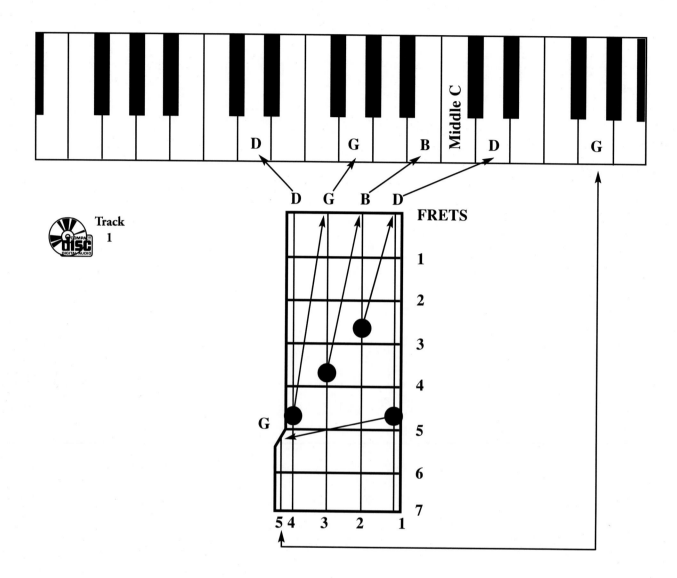

Track 1

If you don't have a piano, here are instructions for the "relative" G tuning of your banjo. Commercially available electronic tuners can also help.

1. Tune the 4th string to D, or anywhere near it. This can be tricky at first, but gets easier as your ear becomes trained.

2. Sound the 4th string with a finger fretting the 5th fret. Tune the 3rd string open to that pitch.

3. Sound the 3rd string with a finger fretting the 4th fret. Tune the 2nd string open to that pitch.

4. Sound the 2nd string with a finger fretting the 3rd fret. Tune the 1st string open to that pitch.

5. Sound the 1st string with a finger fretting the 5th fret. Tune the 5th string open to that pitch.

Left Hand and Right Hand

Left Hand

When you strum a banjo without depressing any of the strings, they vibrate their full length from the nut to the bridge. To change the pitches of the strings, we will actually change the length of the string by pressing the string with the tips of the fingers of the left-hand to the fingerboard at a given fret. This causes the string to rest against a fret wire and vibrate only between the fret that the string is against, and the bridge.

Left-Hand Position

The goal for the left-hand is to be able to move the fingers gracefully, accurately, and quickly to change the lengths of the strings. Each player develops a comfortable posture to hold the banjo neck and also to be in good position to fret the strings in an efficient manner. Cradle the banjo neck between the thumb and forefinger, and position your fingers as shown below. A technique you will need to develop is to keep the fingers arched over the fingerboard in a ready-to-play position so that as the fingertips depress the string(s) intended, they do not touch an adjacent string. This is critical and will come with practice. Be careful to keep up on the ends of the fingers when fretting the strings. As you progress in your playing you will need to develop the technique of fretting with the side of your finger, as when using one finger to fret several strings (called a barre) at once, or when stretching between notes that are several frets apart.

This view shows how the left-hand looks on the fingerboard while playing a C chord.

This view shows how the hand grips the back of the neck for the same chord.

This view shows how the left-hand looks on the fingerboard while playing a D7 chord.

This view shows how the hand grips the back of the neck for the same chord.

Right Hand

Everybody's hand is shaped a little differently and works a little differently. There is an interrelation of the micro-elements of hand position. In the most common hand position, the ring and the little finger of the right-hand rest on the head just below the strings, and near the bridge. There are many fine elements to be concerned with in hand position. The goal is to get the thumb, index finger and middle finger in a comfortable playing position so the tips of the picks are striking the strings in a clean and efficient manner. Much attention should be given to hand position. Watch other players to get an idea of the many variables, and experiment until you find a comfortable position.

Picks

Bluegrass banjo is played by picking the strings with the thumb, index finger and middle finger of the right-hand. Picks are worn on each of those fingers. There are many different styles of both finger picks and thumb picks. The picks you choose will have some degree of effect on tone and comfort, so experiment until you settle on the set that suits you. Watch and talk to other players to get an idea of the variety of choices. My experience is that most players use metal finger picks and a plastic thumb pick. I suggest that you start with that.

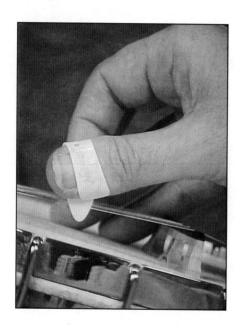

This view shows two fingers resting on the head, just in front of the bridge.

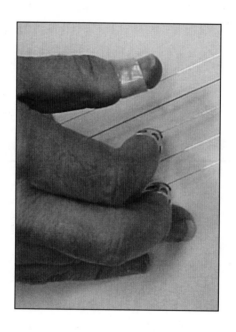

Keep your fingers in line and they will strike each string at the same point.

The goal is to get the thumb, index finger and middle finger in a comfortable playing position so the tips of the picks are striking the strings in a clean and efficient manner.

Chords

A chord is three notes that sound in harmony. Chords provide the background or harmony for melodies and are an important concept to grasp and perform.

Let's first look at the three important chords in the key of G. They are shown below in a chord diagram form. The G chord is the easiest because the form we are using here is sounded by just playing all the strings open. The C chord requires pressing the fingers down in very specific places. Study the chord diagram to insure correct fingering. The same is true for the D7 chord. Note that when you strum across all the strings while holding the D7 chord, the fifth string doesn't sound exactly right. In fact the fifth string, sounding a G, does not fit into a D7 chord, but it is a sound that appears a lot in banjo playing. It is one of the unique things that the five-string banjo has to offer. Get used to it and learn to enjoy it.

Track 2

Left-Hand Fingering:

1 - first finger
2 - second finger
3 - third finger

O = open string

G Chord

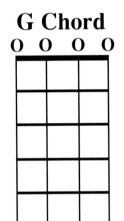

C Chord

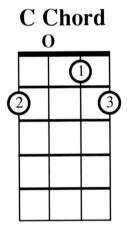

D^7 Chord

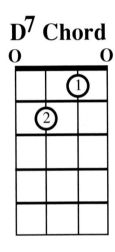

Finger each chord using the fingers shown. Strum across all the strings in each chord and make sure that each note of each chord sounds clearly. The problem you may encounter is that a fretting finger may touch an adjacent string, causing a muted sound. Make slight adjustments with your fingers until you find the best way to place your fingers for the clearest sound. Also, the metal of the strings pressing against the soft flesh of the fingertips causes some pain and discomfort in the beginning. Over time, the fingertips will develop callouses and the pain will go away.

Now we are going to combine fingering the three chords we have learned for the left hand with a picking pattern with our right hand. Much of bluegrass banjo playing is being able to control the fingers of the right hand to hit the strings you want.

First Picking Pattern

The first picking pattern we are going to learn is the single-note-with-pinch pattern. The single note will be picked by the index finger on the second or third or fourth string, as indicated. This is followed by a pinch, which is the thumb sounding the fifth string simultaneously with the middle finger sounding the first string. The rhythm on the single-note pinch pattern is shown above the tablature. It is played evenly, i.e., the distance between each unit of the pattern is equal. Start slowly and work for accuracy and speed. Using a metronome is helpful.

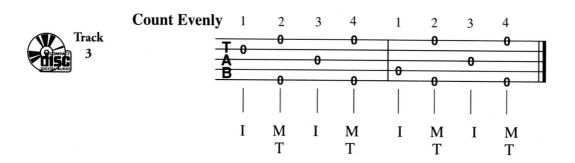

Our next exercise adds the C and D7 chord. As you play through the exercise you may find that you slow down or stop as you reposition the left-hand fingers. This is necessary at first as your fingers learn to dance through the steps required for the changes. At some point you will need to begin to be aggressive about getting your fingers down quickly and accurately. After you have rehearsed and feel you know the fingerings, you may need to throw your fingers at chords and accept the mistakes as you keep the rhythm regular until your fingers have made the micro-muscular adjustments necessary to perform the changes.

Single Note With Pinch

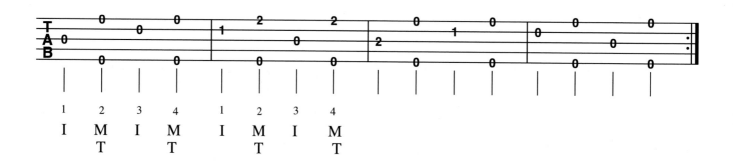

16

Good Night Ladies

The first song we are going to learn in the single-note-with-pinch pattern is "Goodnight Ladies." It uses many of the same movements you have practiced already. The melody notes in this arrangement are the single notes played by the index finger. The pinch supplies a rhythm and adds the harmony notes of the chord. Play just the single notes to hear the main melody alone. Also notice that the melody notes fall on some note of the chord. This is a very common occurrence and will become important as you begin training your ear to hear melodies and chord changes.

Track 4

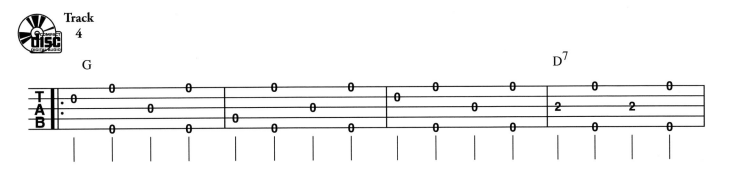

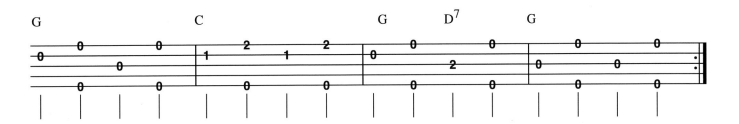

Boil Them Cabbage Down

The next song we are going to learn in the single-note-with-pinch style is "Boil Them Cabbage Down." It uses the same elements of "Good Night Ladies," but arranged in a different sequence. This should give you some clue as to how music, like language, is the simple or highly complex manipulation of a few common sounds.

Track 5

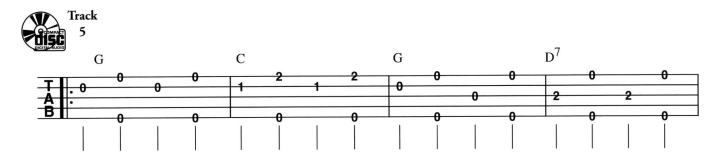

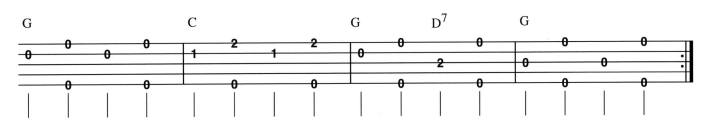

The Slide

Now we are going to add a left-hand technique that gives the music a little more character and makes it a little more song-like. The slide is a technique where a fretted note is picked, and while the note is still sounding, the fretting finger slides to a higher fret. In the example given, the slide is on the third string from the second fret to the fourth fret. Sometimes you will want the slide to be quick and other times slow depending on the effect you want. Practice it both ways.

Examples:
Slide

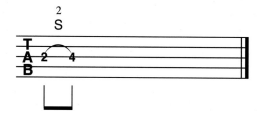

Now let's add the slide to the single-note-with-pinch pattern.

Slide With Pinch

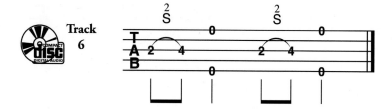

Now lets add this new slide technique to the song "Boil Them Cabbage Down."

Boil Them Cabbage Down (with slide)

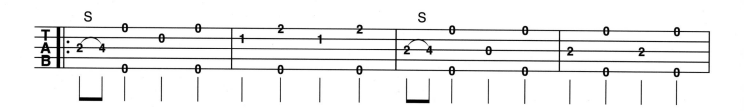

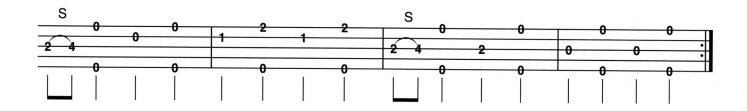

18

The Hammer-on

Another left-hand technique is the hammer-on. On paper the hammer-on looks similar to the slide. It is indicated by a fret number, with a ⌒ to a second higher fret number, and an "H" above the staff line. While the open string is still sounding, a finger is brought down (hammered) on the string at the higher fret.

Example

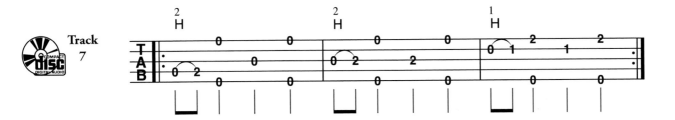

Let's add both the slide and the hammer-on to "Boil Them Cabbage Down".

Boil Them Cabbage Down (with slide and hammer-on)

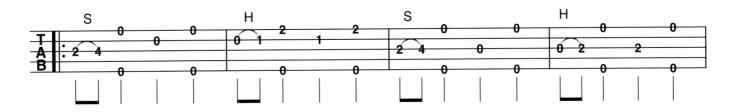

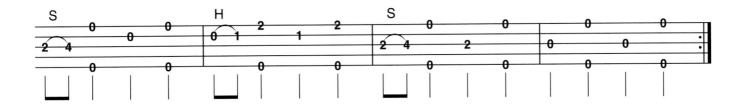

Practice until you can perform these left-hand techniques smoothly. Increase the tempo as you feel comfortable. You will notice that as the tempo increases, the execution of the slide and hammer-on has to be a little quicker.

Practice Tip

In order to get a good sense of your right and left-hand positions, play looking into a mirror. Turn several different ways to get different views into your right-hand position. Work towards playing on the tips of your picks. Avoid digging too deeply into the strings. Many beginning players hit the banjo head with their picks and causes and non-rhythmical and nonmusical sound. Make sure you have a slight bend in your wrist. As you use your left-hand fingers to fret the strings, work to keep them close to the fingerboard just above the strings. Pay attention to both hands and work towards smooth, graceful, and efficient finger movements.

The Roll

The essence of banjo picking is the concept of the thumb, index finger and middle finger playing in arpeggio patterns; that is, single notes played in rapid succession. The basic bluegrass banjo style divides a measure of 4/4 into eight equally spaced notes.

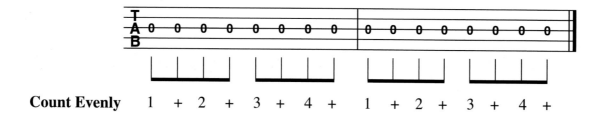

Count Evenly   1   +   2   +   3   +   4   +   1   +   2   +   3   +   4   +

The style is further characterized by how the three picking fingers combine to produce the eight-note patterns or rolls. There are three basic finger movements, which are assigned directional names (forward, backward) and a descriptive name (alternating).

Forward - T (thumb)	**I (index)**	**M (middle)**	
Backward - M (middle)	**I (index)**	**T (thumb)**	
Alternating - T (thumb)	**I (index)**	**T (thumb)**	**M (middle)**
(also MIMT)			

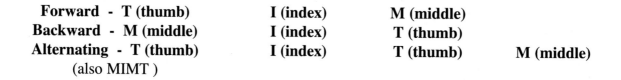

We are going to move slowly into using rolls by combining a four-note roll for a half measure, with the single-note pinch we learned for the second half of the measure.

Four-Note Roll With Single Note and Pinch

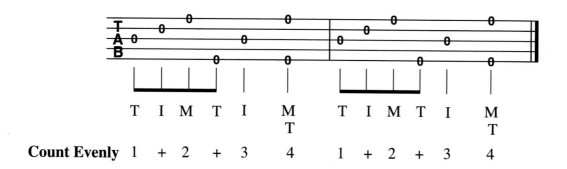

Count Evenly 1   +   2   +   3   4   1   +   2   +   3   4

20

As you play through this pattern, be sure to sound the measure as indicated. It is very important that you perform the roll with the proper timing. When you feel comfortable with the roll, gradually increase the tempo.

Now perform the roll with the G, C, D7 chords you have learned.

Track
9

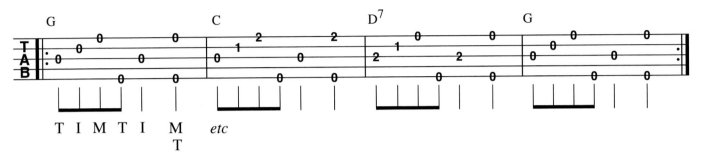

It is important to realize that a roll is the order in which the fingers move and not necessarily the strings they hit. The tablature may indicate different strings, but the order of the picking fingers is the same.

Track
10

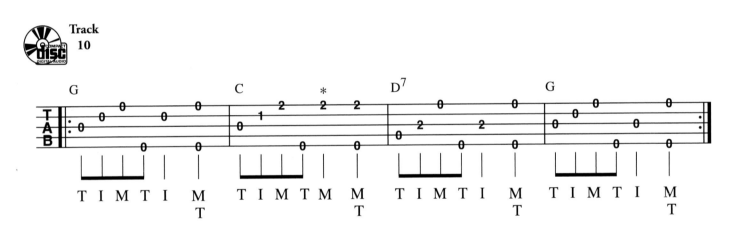

It is important to take time at this point to make sure your timing is correct, that you are hitting the strings cleanly and clearly, that the slides and hammer-ons are crisp, and that the sound you are getting is a pleasant sound. No matter what your level of skill, know your material well and make your playing sound the best it can. Listen to good players and strive to imitate their good sounds.

Now we are going to incorporate this new picking pattern with left-hand movements we have already learned and play a new version of "Boil Them Cabbage Down" and "Good Night Ladies."

This is a slight variation in that the middle finger is striking the single note rather than the index finger.

Track 11

Boil Them Cabbage Down

(with four-note roll, single note, pinch, slide and hammer-on)

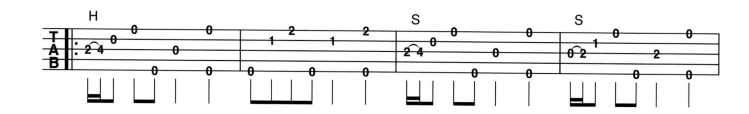

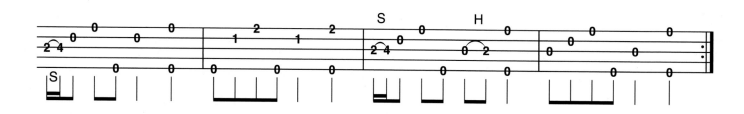

Track 12

Good Night Ladies

(with four-note roll, single note, pinch, slide and hammer-on)

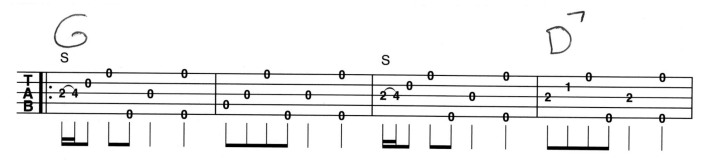

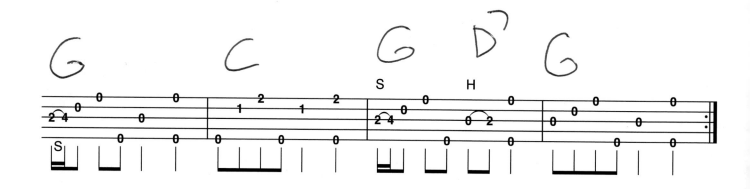

"Cumberland Gap" is another popular banjo tune you can play using the techniques you have learned. Note that in the last half of the second measure, the single note before the pinch is on the first string. In the last half of the third measure there are two single notes and no pinch. Also note the first and last measures are the same. Just as in language, where words are repeated and repositioned, musical phrases are repeated and repositioned. Watch and listen for phrases that are the same or very similar.

Track 13

Cumberland Gap

(with four-note roll, single note, pinch, slide and hammer-on)

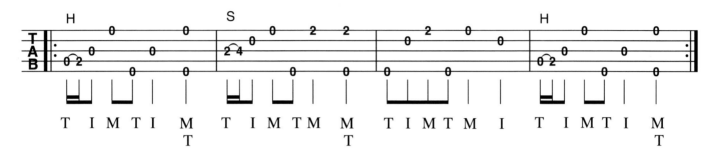

The Alternating Roll

The next roll pattern we are going to learn has come to have several names: square roll, alternating roll, or thumb-in-and-out roll. The idea behind the alternating roll is that the thumb alternates between the index and middle fingers in a four-note pattern. This four-note pattern of eighth notes may be repeated twice to fill a four/four measure.

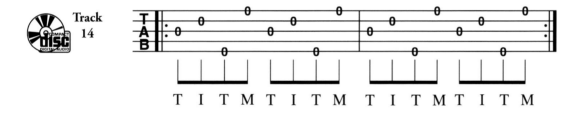
Track 14

In the example above, the thumb plays the third string and the fifth string. Rolls are the order of the right-hand fingers, not necessarily the strings they strike. Below are two examples of other ways the alternating roll is used, striking different combinations of strings.

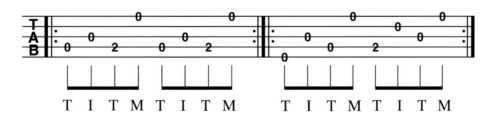

Remember we will be adding left-hand fretted notes that will give the different combinations more meaning. Here are a few common alternating roll passages for you to practice.

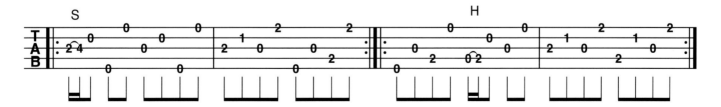

Let's use this new pattern to play the old favorite "Boil Them Cabbage Down." With this new version, we will add a new C position.

New "C" Position

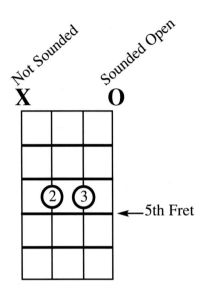

The reason this is still a C chord is that we have moved the C and E notes of the C chord to a new place on the neck. (Play the first two strings of the first C-chord position and compare them with the third and second strings of the new C-chord position, and hear that they are the same notes.) In "Boil Them Cabbage Down" the C note is the melody note we want in the second measure. In the first C-chord position, the C note is on the second string. The alternating roll as we have outlined, has to have two strings above the melody string. The new C-chord position has the C note on the third string. This is an important concept to grasp, because when you begin arranging melodies in the bluegrass style, you will need to have the ability to find the same melody note at several locations on the neck in order to match them with particular rolls.

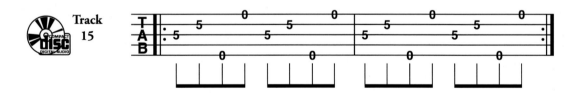

Here is the alternating roll with the new C-chord position. You will note that the open first string D note is sounded. It is not part of the C chord but adds what is referred to as an "added ninth." It adds an openness, or expanded sound, to the chord, which is an interesting and beautiful sound often used in bluegrass.

Here is "Boil Them Cabbage Down" using the alternating roll coupled with slides, hammer-ons, and the new C-chord position.

Boil Them Cabbage Down

Track 16

(alternating roll with slides and new C position)

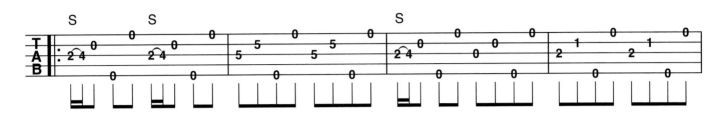

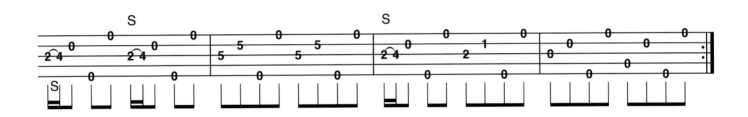

Here is "Good Night Ladies" using the alternating roll with slides, hammer-ons and the new C-chord position.

Good Night Ladies

Track 17

(alternating roll with slides, hammer-on and new C position)

25

Cripple Creek

Here is a neat arrangement of the classic banjo tune "Cripple Creek" that utilizes all the techniques we have discussed up to this point: the single-note-with-pinch, four-note roll and alternating roll, coupled with slides and the new C-chord position. Note that we are changing the 2-4, third-string slide to a 2-3 slide.

Cripple Creek   A A B B

(with single-note-and-pinch, four-note roll, alternating roll with slides.)

The Forward Roll

At the heart of bluegrass banjo playing is a group of rolls known as "forward rolls." These rolls are the more syncopated rolls in that the melodies often fall in slightly unusual places in the measure. Often melodies fall on what is sometimes referred to as the strong part of the beat, i.e, the down beats 1 2 3 or 4. When a melody note is shifted from the strong position to what is referred to as the weak part of the beat, i.e., the up-beat, or the "and" of the beat, as in "1 and 2 and 3 and 4 and," the melody has been syncopated. The forward rolls have the capacity to do this. Forward rolls are usually organized by patterns of two–three–three or three–three–two to create an eight-note pattern. The first example we will look at is **(TM) (TIM) (TIM)**.
                                                                                                      2   3   3

Forward Rolls

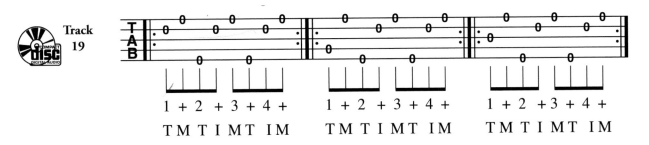

The easiest way to learn the pattern is to remember that the thumb and middle finger play the first component, followed by two patterns of thumb-index-middle. Practice this pattern until it flows smoothly and seamlessly from one repetition to the next.

Remember that a roll is the order that the fingers move and not what strings they hit. You will need to practice the patterns with the fingers striking different strings. The example below will demonstrate this. Note that the finger order of the right-hand is the same each time; the difference is the strings they strike.

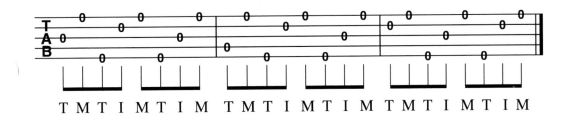

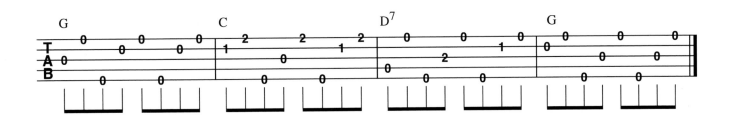

27

Let's use the forward roll to play "Boil Them Cabbage Down" and "Good Night Ladies."

Boil Them Cabbage Down

(with forward roll)

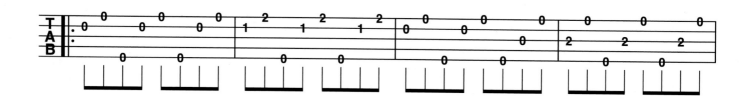

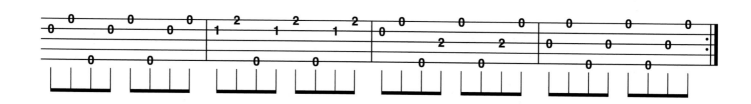

Good Night Ladies

(with forward roll)

Now that we have a number of right-hand roll patterns and left-hand techniques to work with, let's put them into a version of our old standby "Boil Them Cabbage Down."

Track
22

Boil Them Cabbage Down

(with mixed rolls and slides)

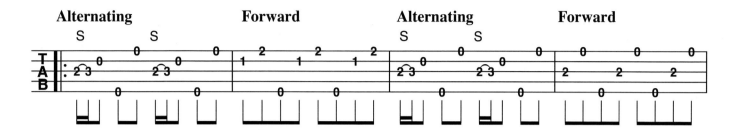

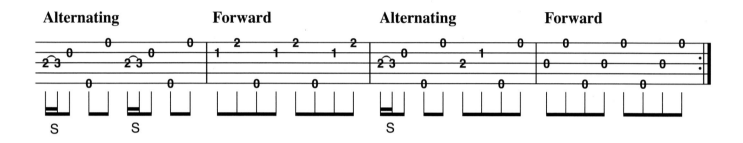

Forward/Backward Roll

The "forward/backward" roll (also referred to as forward/reverse roll) has two sections to it, as its name suggests. There is a forward roll (T I M), the thumb then strikes the fifth string, a backward roll (M I T), ending with the middle finger striking the first string.

Track
23

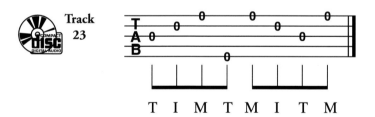

As with all roll patterns, the order in which the fingers move is the key. The strings that are struck can be altered to create the note order you want.

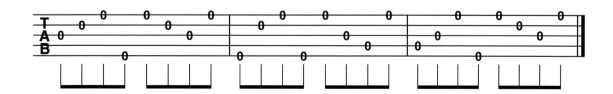

Let's use this new pattern to play a variation of "Cripple Creek."

Note that there is a new left-hand fingering position introduced in the first measure, and another new position in the fifth measure. Practice that measure until you feel comfortable with the movement and coordination of the two hands. The A section of the tune uses three forward/backward rolls in the first three measures, and the last measure is a four-note roll with a single note and pinch.

A neat thing about the forward/backward roll is that a left-hand position can be held on the first half of the roll and then changed or released on the second half of the roll, as in the first three measures of this new arrangement of "Cripple Creek."

Track
24

Cripple Creek

(with forward/backward roll)

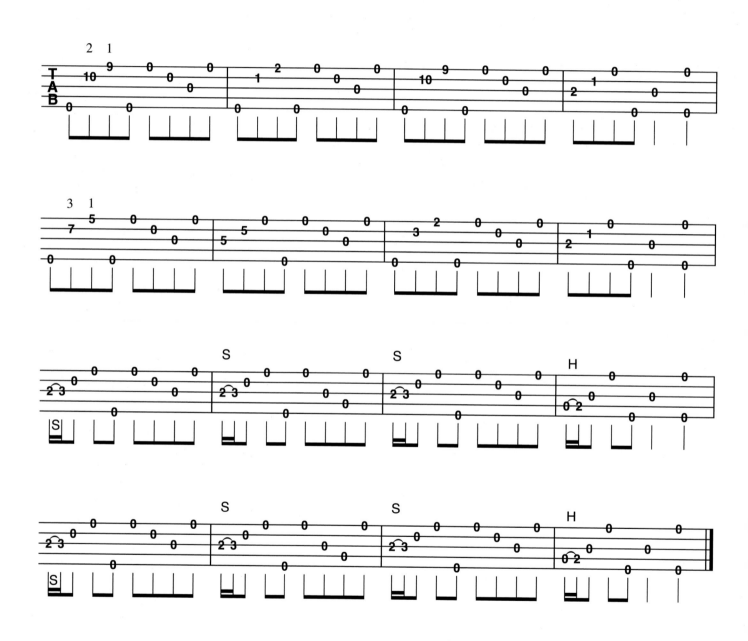

The Pull-off

An important left-hand technique is the pull-off. In this technique, a finger of the left hand actually plucks the string in addition to the string being plucked by a finger of the right hand. The pull-off should not be viewed as merely a lift-off of the finger, but a vigorous pull with the finger.

Example #1 is a pull-off from the second fret, first string, to the open first string. With your second finger at the second fret, pluck the string with the middle finger of the right-hand. As the string is sounding, pluck the first string with the second finger of the left hand. The left-hand finger executing the pull-off is the same finger that is fretting the string. The direction of the left-hand pull-off will be down towards the ground.

Example #1

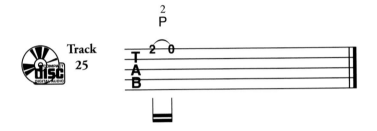

Exercise #1 uses the pull-off in a roll situation. Practice until you are comfortable with the sound and feel.

Exercise #1

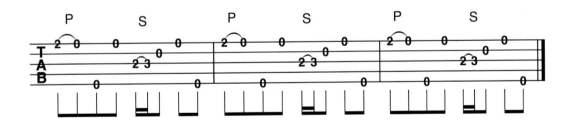

Example #2 is a commonly used pull-off and is a prominent component in many phrases of bluegrass banjo playing. Notice the note that is sounded first is the third string, third fret. The pull-off is to the third string, second fret. This is performed by the second finger fretting the third string at the third fret, pulling-off to the first finger fretting the second fret. It is not uncommon for players to actually push-off, so to speak, with the plucking finger of the left hand pushing up or towards the ceiling. Whether you pull to the ground or push to the ceiling on this particular maneuver, you must pluck the string again with the left-hand finger.

Example #2

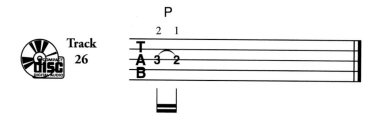

Exercise #2 utilizes this 3-2 pull-off in the context of a forward/backward roll. This phrase is put to good use in later material in the book.

Exercise #2

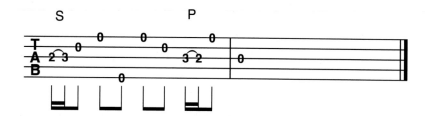

Practice Tip

One way to get your rolls up to speed is to play along with recorded music. Even if you do not know the piece, you can mute the strings and play rolls in rhythm with the recording. The banjo at its basic level is that of a harmonic drummer. Take away the harmony by muting the strings, and you can perfect the rhythm function of your playing. Your fingers can get a sense of the groove that music requires. This also works well with a metronome or a drum machine.

Train 45 Roll

The next pattern is not quite as orderly as the patterns we have learned up to now. It is the defining roll pattern in "Train 45" and is similar to the opening statement of "Foggy Mountain Breakdown."

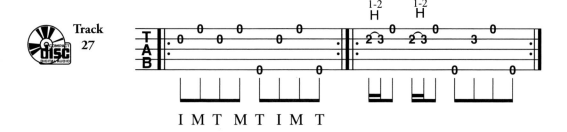

I M T M T I M T

Modified Forward/Backward Roll

Another roll pattern that is similar to a forward/backward roll but different, i.e., sort of a half forward/backward, is shown below. It is used quite a bit and is the roll used to do what I call "The Lick." It is probably the most-used passage in all bluegrass banjo playing. It is the banjo players' equivalent to the Lester Flatt "G-Run" for guitar players. Again, let's put all you have just learned into a really great-sounding bluegrass-styled instrumental called "Levelland Mountain Breakdown." You will need to learn a new chord position. It is a standard position and can be used as a moveable chord (one that does not have any open strings). In this instance it is used as an F chord. Learn that new chord position and then move on to learn the tune.

"The Lick"

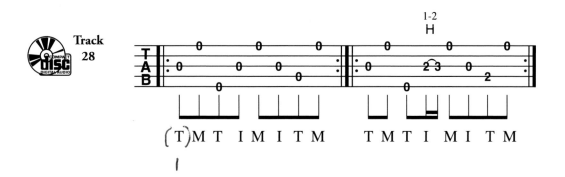

(T) M T I M I T M   T M T I M I T M

F Chord

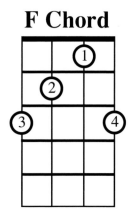

33

Levelland Mountain Breakdown

Here is a piece that pulls together many of the techniques covered in this section. Work diligently to put it all together.

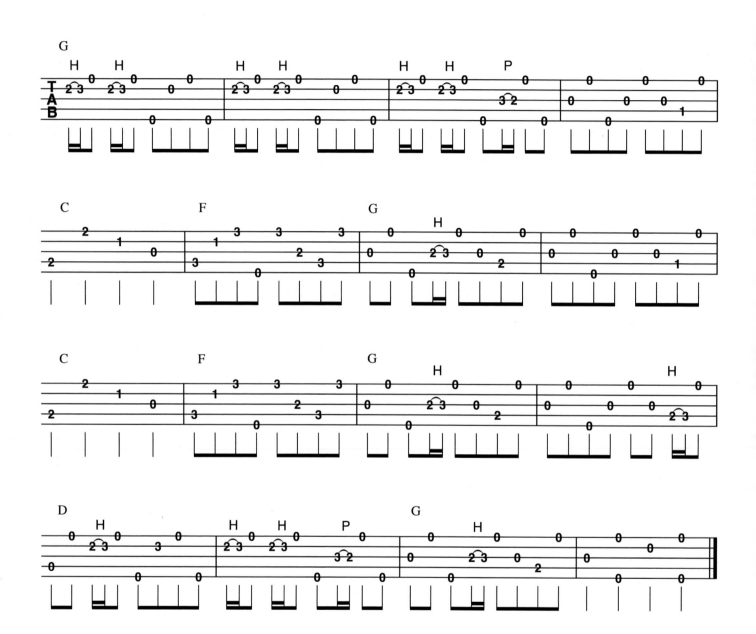

Practice Tip

Many good practice strategies exist. One thing to remember in all of them is that you want to achieve certain goals: making cleaner pull-offs, making smoother rolls, and learning a new passage. If you have a goal that is contained in a short phrase, practice just that for three minutes straight. If you do not get it, lengthen the time to six minutes. It is important to take small, successful steps.

Guidelines for Determining Right-Hand Fingerings

There is a logical way to determine which fingers to use in the picking patterns presented here. In the system used in this book, the following is generally true.

Guideline #1

- The first string is picked by the middle finger*.

- The second string can be picked either by the index finger or thumb.

- The third string can be picked by either by the index finger or the thumb.

- The thumb picks the fourth string. (I have a bias against the index finger picking the fourth string as part of a roll pattern. The index finger will pick the fourth string in the single-string style presented in Tools and Techniques.)

- The thumb picks the fifth string.

- Here is a quick reference:

Picking Finger	String(s) Picked
M	1st*
I	2nd and 3rd
T	5th, 4th, 3rd, 2nd

Guideline #2

- The same finger generally cannot pick consecutive eighth notes in a roll. (At slow tempos it can be done, but as the tempos increase it becomes less do-able. There are those players that can pick consecutive eighth notes with the same finger, as part of a special musical and technical presentation, but in general it is not done.)

There are occasions when the middle finger will be used to pluck the second string in a roll pattern. It is often referred to as an inside roll. It is used in this book only on one occasion- #7f of the "Solos to Songs" section.

35

Fingering Examples

Example #1 shows two measures of a forward roll. The first measure can start with either the thumb (my preference) or the index finger. Since the first measure ends with the middle finger, the second measure can again begin with either the thumb (my preference) or index finger.

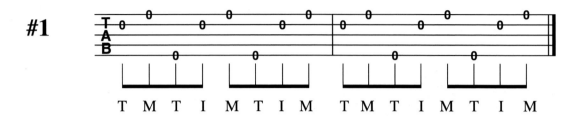

Example #2 shows the first measure as the Train 45 roll. Since it ends with the thumb, the index finger must start the next measure (Guideline #1 and #2).

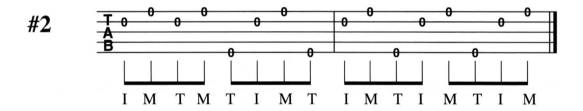

Example #3 shows the first measure as a forward roll and the second measure as the Train 45 roll. The first measure ends with the middle finger, so the next measure could start with either the thumb (my preference) or the index finger, which is the finger that is often used in this roll. Additionally, the third note in the second measure may be picked with the thumb (my preference) or the index finger.

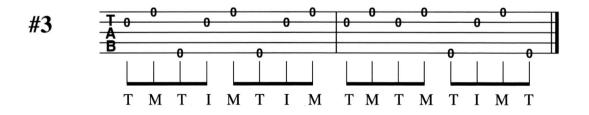

Guideline #3

Following guidelines #1 and #2, consecutive quarter notes can be picked by the same finger, as in example # 4 below. Alternating the thumb and index finger is an option, but not required.

#4

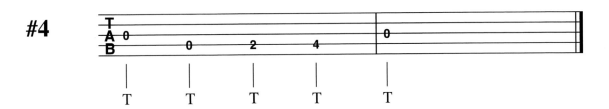

Example #5 is a roll ending with the thumb, so the first quarter note, which is an eighth note away, must be picked by the index finger.

#5

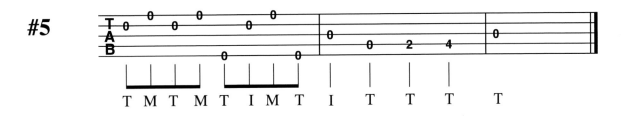

Example #6 demonstrates that the first note, a quarter note, can be picked with the thumb, followed by the thumb picking the fifth string.

#6

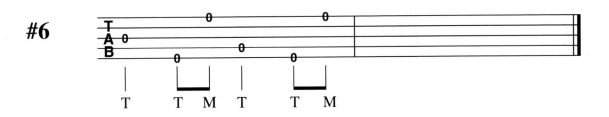

This all may seem complicated but will become clearer as your speed increases and it becomes more difficult to pick consecutive eighth notes with the same finger. It can be a big stumbling block. If the situation is analyzed using the guidelines, the problem can be solved. Once solved, it becomes easier to see the logic in the fingering choices.

37

SECTION 2: Review of Rolls, New Rolls, and Combinations of Rolls, With Examples

This section is a review of the rolls learned in the "Getting Started" section, plus new rolls and combinations of rolls. Each roll is numbered and followed by a number of examples of its use. The examples shown are commonly played phrases that appear with great frequency in bluegrass banjo playing. These examples should be practiced until they become physical and musical gestures that come easily to your fingers and to your ear. There are many variations and combinations of rolls used by players, and the rolls here represent only some of the more commonly played ones. In each of these you should strive to gain control of your fingers so they can move in any picking pattern that the music and style calls for. This takes a lot of disciplined practice.

1. Review of Rolls

Example #1 is the four-note roll with single note and pinch (the first roll presented in the earlier section). Example #1e is the banjo's attempt to duplicate the musical introduction that fiddle players often use to set the timing of a piece; it is sometimes referred to as "potatoes."

Track 30

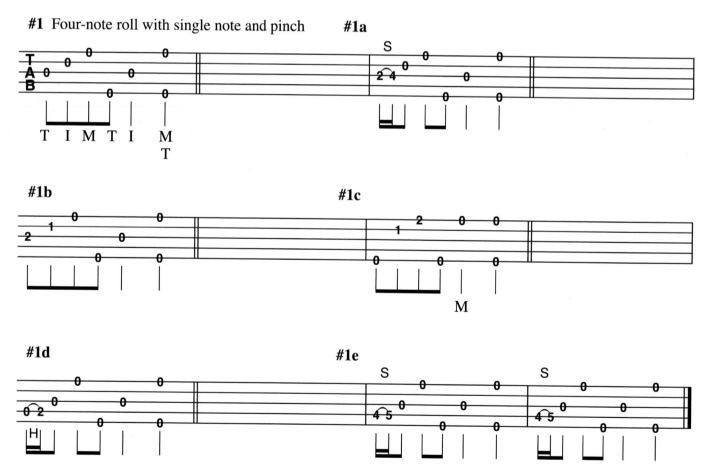

38

2. Alternating Rolls

Example #2 is the alternating pattern. This relatively straightforward roll is used in many circumstances that may not be apparent to a beginner. This roll produces the sound of #2a, which should be familiar as part of the "Cripple Creek" chorus. By changing the strings struck by the fingers, you can also produce the phrases demonstrated in the remaining examples. Notice in #2c that the fifth note of the pattern is the fifth string. By sounding the fifth string in this spot, which is the downbeat and usually the place for a melody note, it displaces the emphasis and creates syncopation in the melody. It is used often and should be learned well. This is also true in #2d, but here the fifth string is the first note of the pattern. Remember that the roll pattern is the order in which the fingers move, not the strings they hit.

Track 31

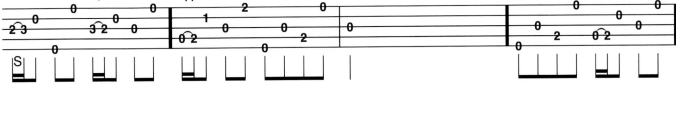

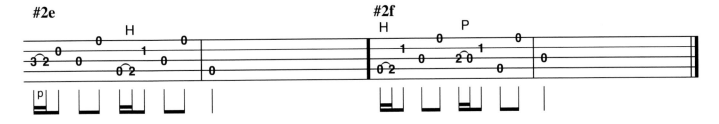

39

3. Forward/Backward Roll

Example #3 is the forward/backward roll. Examples #3a and #3d are two of the most widely used phrases in all of bluegrass banjo playing. Spend time learning these two rolls and listen for their use by your favorite players. The logic of this roll divides the measure into two parts separated by the open fifth string. This allows you to have one chord, or position of notes, fingered with the left-hand on the first half of the measure, and to switch smoothly to a different position on the second half of the measure as the fifth string is sounded. In #3c there are two different chords in each measure. In bluegrass banjo playing, an open string is often required for making smooth transitions with the left-hand. When an open string is not available, as at the end of each measure in #3c, you have to move quickly. Sometimes you have to move so quickly at fast tempos that the last note of a roll actually sounds the note of the next position. This may seem complicated, but in fact it is a happenstance of the roll streaming and the left-hand changing positions at fast tempos. Example #3d is a variation of #3a.

Track
32

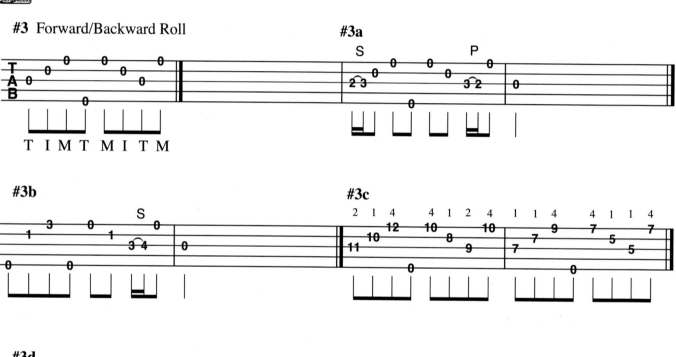

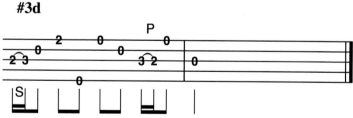

40

4. Variations of the Forward Roll

We learned a version of the forward roll in the first section. Examples #4.1 through #4.3c illustrate some variations of that roll. The roll we learned has the TM TIM TIM finger order. The one listed as #4.2 moves the two-note portion of the roll to the end of the measure so that it becomes TIM TIM TM. #4.3 is M TIM TIM T, which splits the two-note portion of the roll and places one note at each end of the measure.

Track 33

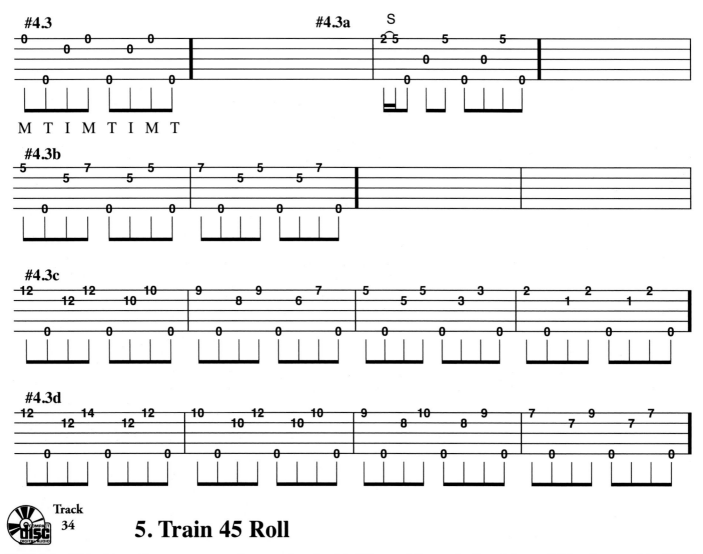

Track 34

5. Train 45 Roll

Example #5 is the roll most commonly associated with "Foggy Mountain Breakdown." It's also used in "Train 45," another popular banjo showpiece (see SONGS section). Example #5a features two hammer-ons in the first half of the measure. Example #5b plays the first note, the D on the second string/third fret, straight on, with no hammer-on. Note that the second note of the roll is omitted. Example #5c will take some work, as it has the two hammer-ons and a pull-off. This phrase is used quite a bit, so give it your full and careful attention.

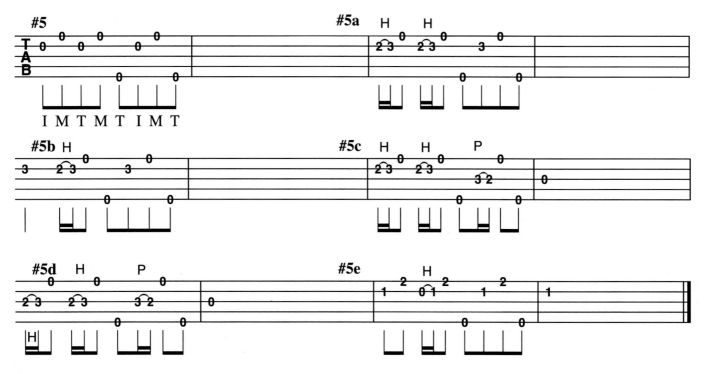

6. Modified Forward/Backward Roll

I refer to this roll as a modified forward/backward roll. I call #6a "The Lick." It is used a lot as a punctuation mark at the ends of phrases, or as a fill-in lick to take up musical space. It is comparable to the G-run in bluegrass guitar. I'm sure that after you play it and listen to it you'll realize that you've heard it a great deal in your favorite bluegrass recordings. Example #6c is also a good fill-in figure that can be played repeatedly as you wait for the singer to come in.

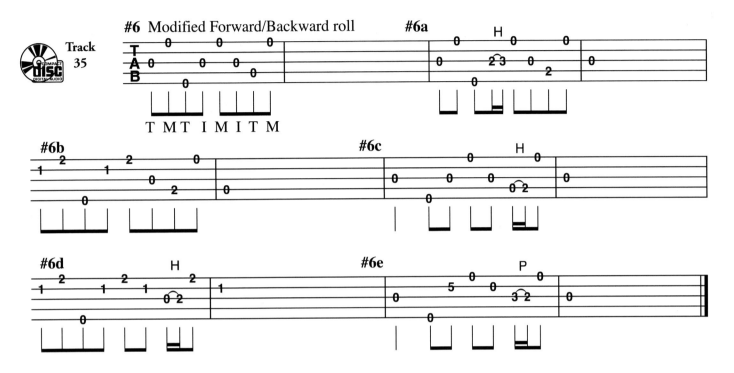

New Rolls

Now that you've had time to get control of your fingers through careful study and practice of the "Getting Started" and "Review of Rolls" sections, let's look at some new rolls.

7. Reno Roll

Example #7 is a roll featured effectively in the music of Don Reno. In this Reno Roll, #7a, the open first string (the third and sixth note of the roll) is where the left-hand position shift occurs on the fourth and/or eighth note of the roll. In example #7b, the last note of the roll before the position change is played open in order to facilitate a smooth transition. As you play through these examples it should become clear how the roll and the position shifts are operating.

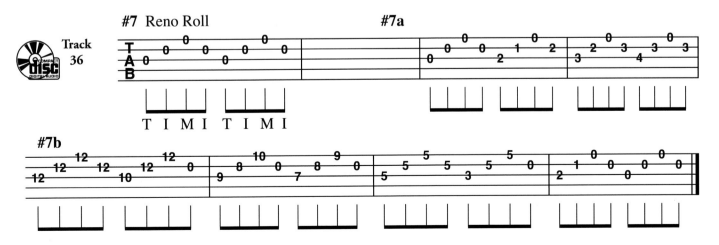

8. Timing Fill-in Lick

Example #8 is basically a timing fill-in lick that is often used as the equivalent of a single note and pinch. Played once, it takes a half measure, so it is often played in conjunction with another half-measure roll to make a full measure, as in #8a and #8b. Bluegrass banjo playing is a contemporary expression of American folk instrumental playing and draws on many previous styles. This small T TM roll can also be used as a complete style of playing, as in the song "Ground Hog," included in the SONGS section.

Examples

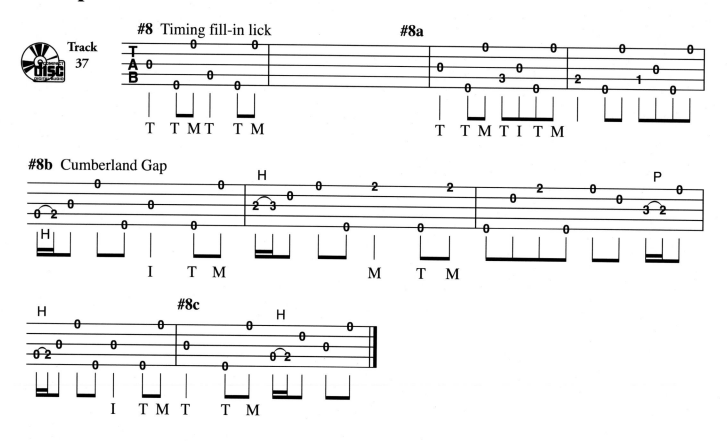

#9. Four-String Forward Roll

Example #9 is a roll I use to play the fourth to first string. The fingering pattern is an alternating pattern, TITM, with the thumb crossing to the second string on the third and seventh notes of the pattern.
Example #9b is a pattern that results in a sweeping arpeggio across a chord.

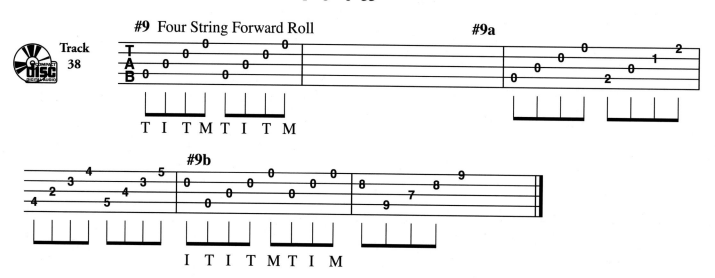

10. Four-String Backward Roll

Track 39

Example #10 is the reverse of Example #9, and again, is an alternating pattern, this time beginning with the middle finger, MTIT.

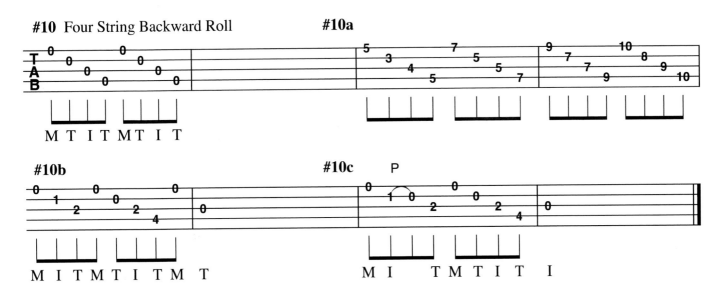

Combinations of Rolls

Rolls are often combined to create phrases longer than just one measure or less. Below are some of the more common combinations.

11. Four Patterns of TIM and 4-Note Alternating Pattern

Example #11 combines four patterns of TIM, for a total of twelve eighth notes, and then a four-note alternating pattern, TITM, at the end, for a total of sixteen eighth notes to fill the two measures. Example #11a shows how it might be used over a G chord and a C chord as an accompaniment idea. Example #11b demonstrates the roll combination used to play a standard bluegrass melody. To complete the melodic idea, I've added the last two measures with the rolls indicated. Example #11c is often used over a D chord, and then walks up to the G note of the G chord.

Track 40

11. Four Patterns of TIM and 4-Note Alternating Pattern

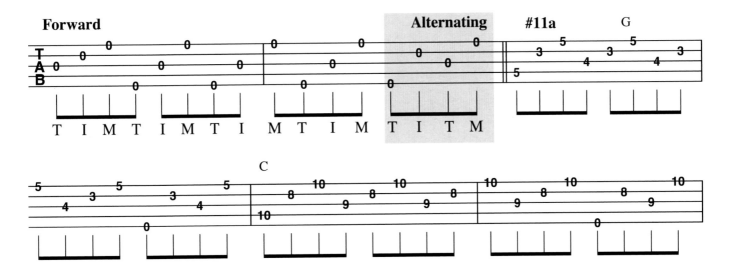

45

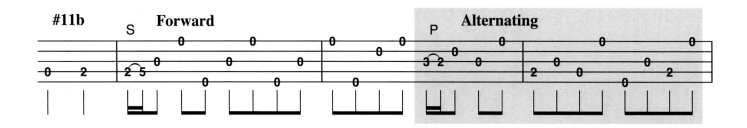

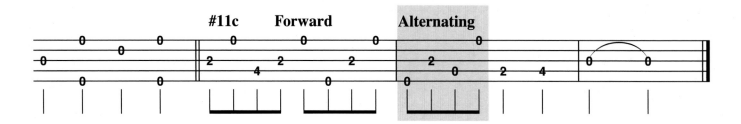

12. Train 45 Roll, Alternating Pattern, and Backward Roll

Example #12 is the combination of the Train 45 roll, an alternating pattern, and a backward roll. Examples #12a and #12b are very similar but begin on different strings. Note that in #12b, the second note of the roll, the D note on the first string, is omitted. This is not an uncommon practice. Study the arrangements in the SONGS section for examples of notes left out of a roll.

Track
41

#12 Train 45 roll, alternating pattern, and backward roll

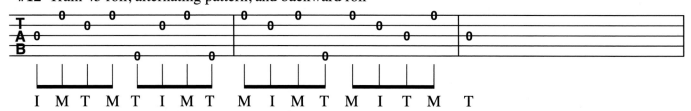

I M T M T I M T   M I M T M I T M T

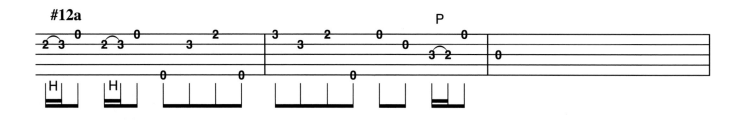

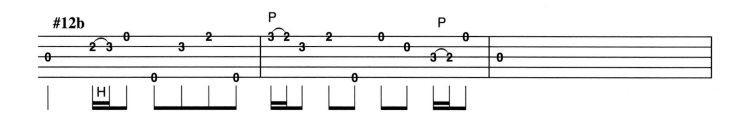

46

13. Alternating Pattern and Forward Roll

Example #13 is the combination of an alternating pattern and a forward roll in one measure. Example #13a is a phrase that leads to the C note of the C chord, or it might lead to the D note, (shown in parentheses). Example #13b is also an alternating pattern combined with a four-note forward roll; it works nicely as an ending phrase.

Track 42

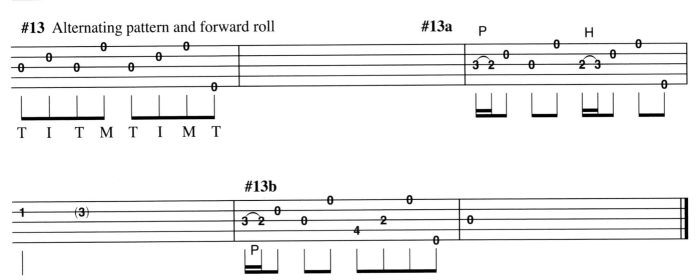

Track 43 (Insert Your Name Here) Breakdown

Here is an exercise for practicing some of the phrases you have learned in the context of a commonly played bluegrass chord progression. Over each measure is the number and letter of the choice of phrase, taken from the examples in this section. You should explore and find others that also fit.

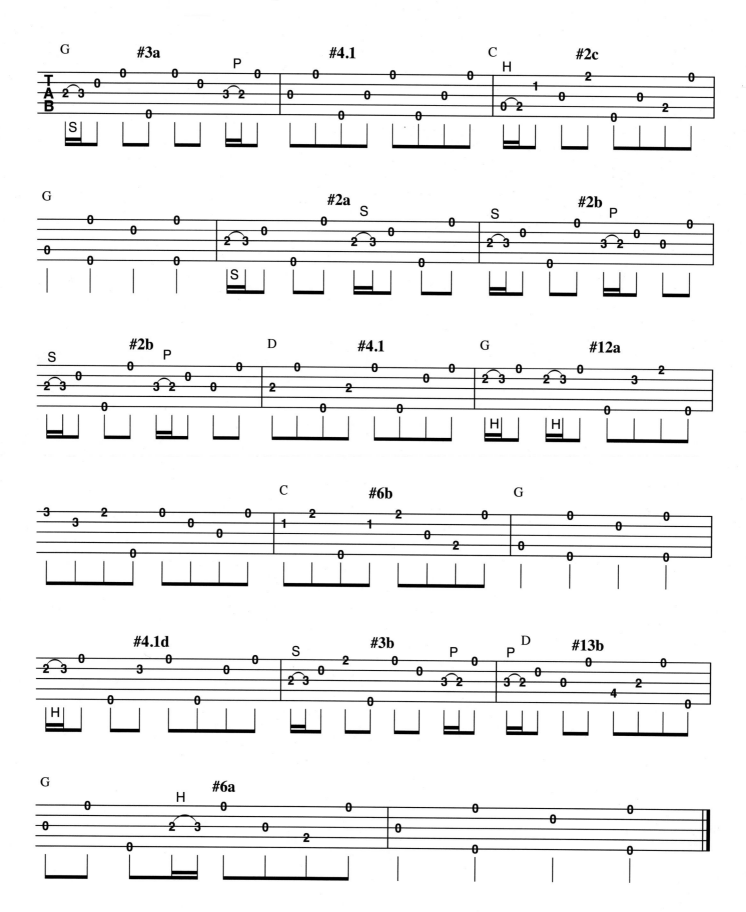

48

SECTION 3: Roll Logic

An important characteristic of bluegrass banjo playing is the fitting of melodies – usually with one, two, three, or four notes per measure – into the many different roll patterns, usually eight notes per measure.

Each roll features a different placement of the melody notes within the roll. Along with the melody note placement, each roll features a different placement of the harmony notes (notes that are not the melody) within the roll. A few similar rolls place the melody notes in the same position, but the position of the harmony notes is different with each roll. Along with understanding rolls, and melody and harmony placement, is the decision about where the melody note will be played. For instance, the G note of the fifth string can be played on the first string at the fifth fret, the second string at the eighth fret, the third string at the twelfth fret, or the fourth string at the seventeenth fret, as in Example #1. Each option would change the roll choices and, in turn, the sound of the melody note (in this case, G), and the position of that note in the rest of the chord. Depending on the choice of the melody note (on the first, second, third, or fourth string), the harmony notes could be above or below the melody. This will become more apparent as you work through the following material.

Example #1

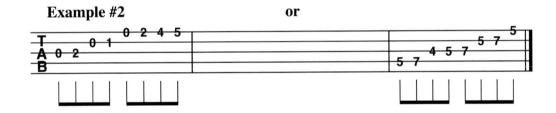

Melodies and harmonies are derived from scales. Many times, scales are in a form that moves across the strings, as in Example #2. While it's useful to learn as many different fingerings as you can imagine for all the scales, for our purposes we'll view them as being fingered up and down a single string at a time. Later, these scales on each string can be combined in more playable ways.

Example #2   or

For the examples we'll use the G scale, the key most often used by bluegrass banjo players. We'll begin with the notes of the G scale fretted on the first string. For now, fret each note with the second finger. As you perform more complicated music, you'll need to develop a more sophisticated fingering system.

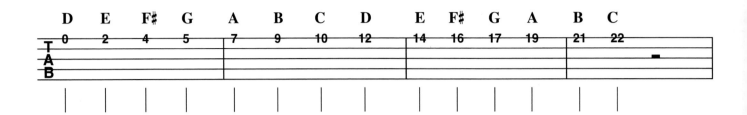

First String

Roll #1 is designed to place a melody on the first string. Note that in this roll the first string appears three times – on the first, fourth and seventh notes of the roll. All are places a melody note can be played. We don't have a melody, so for now we'll use the notes of the G scale on the first string.

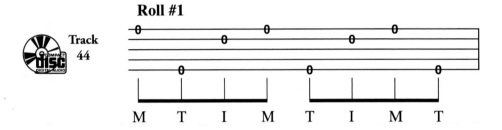

In Example #1a the scale is played in combination with the roll. Listen to the rhythm of the fretted notes and also to the sound of those notes against the open strings. As you learn more in later sections, we'll add fretted notes to the open strings. The fifth string will usually be played open.

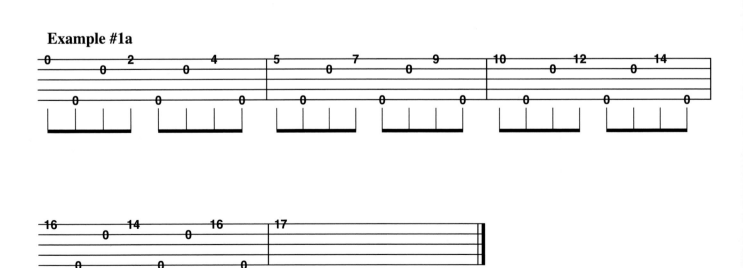

Example #1b uses the fretted notes to create a descending musical idea.

Example #1b

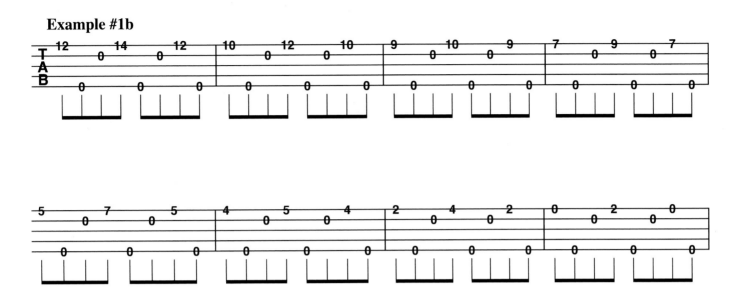

Improvising can be thought of as creating a new melody. As you become comfortable with the above examples, try creating your own melodies by combining the fretted notes with the roll. Leap around to different G-scale notes on the first string as you play the roll. Create a melody. Find a melody to a commonly known song, such as "Bury Me Beneath the Willow" or "Grandfather's Clock," and try to make them work within the context of the roll in Example #1. For now, just work on fitting the melody into the roll. As you play through these ideas, they may sound a bit awkward, as we've not added any chord changes to the melody. Later we'll add harmony, or the chords, to songs.

Roll #2 is another roll for melodies on the first string. It's a form of the alternating roll. In this roll the picking pattern is MIMT MIMT. Some players use their thumb instead of the index finger in this roll, so that it is MTMT MTMT. Try both ways and decide which you prefer. In this roll the first string appears four times, and as a result, offers the opportunity to play more melody notes. Roll #1 syncopates the melody. Syncopation is the distinctive sound that results from playing a melody note on the weak part of the beat. The strong beats are 1, 2, 3, 4, while the weak part of the beat is the "and," or "up" part, as in "1-and-2-and-3-and-4-and." In Roll #1, the fourth note of the roll (the second time the first string is sounded) carries the melody but is on the "and" or "up" beat. In Roll #2 all the melody notes on the first string are on the strong beats, and so are not syncopated. This is an important distinction.

Roll #2

Track 45

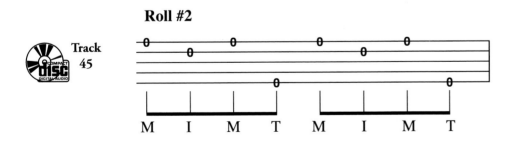

M   I   M   T   M   I   M   T

Example #2a is an ascending line combining the roll and, again, the notes of the G scale on the first string.

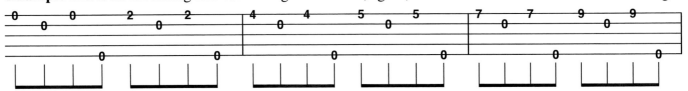

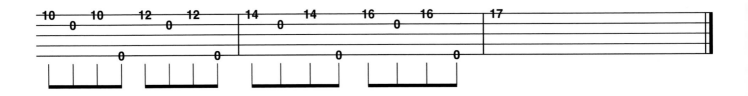

Example #2b is a descending idea, as in #1b.

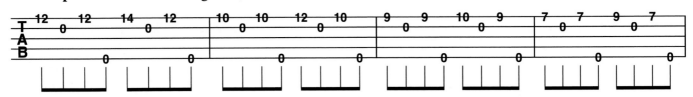

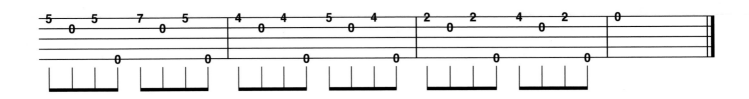

Create your own melody by selecting notes in an order that's pleasing or interesting to you.

Second String

We'll use the same approach with the second string. First, locate the notes of the G scale on the second string.

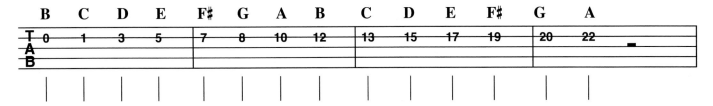

Roll #1 is a roll that carries the melody on the second string. Note that the second string appears three times in this roll – that's three opportunities for melody notes.

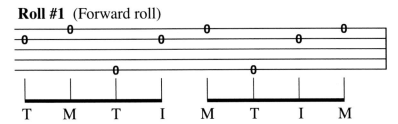

Example #1a couples the roll with the ascending scale. Notice that I've put a scale note at each second-string opportunity in the roll. This is just a place to start. Again, what you should do is create your own melody. Try as many possibilities as you can imagine, of combining the roll and the scale.

Example #1a

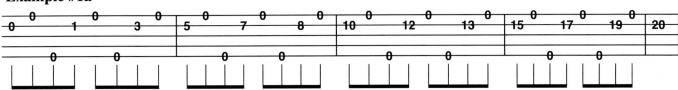

Example #1b is a descending melodic idea (as in First String #1b).

Example #1b

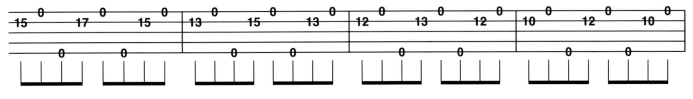

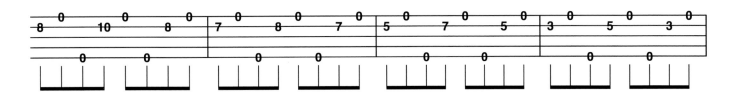

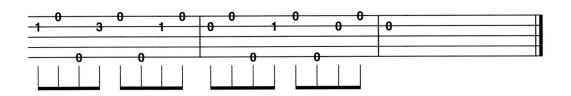

Roll #2 is another roll that's often used to play a melody on the second string. In Getting Started, I referred to this roll as the Train 45 roll. The second string appears three times in this roll. In another roll, however, depending on where and how many times the second string appears, the rhythm of the melody will change.

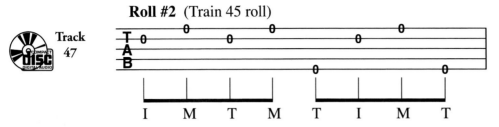

Example #2a expresses an ascending scale idea.

Example #2a

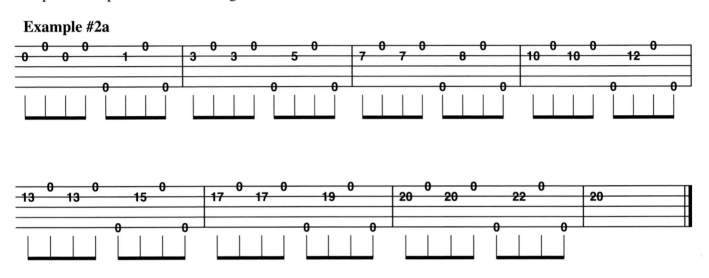

Example #2b expresses a descending scale idea.

Example #2b

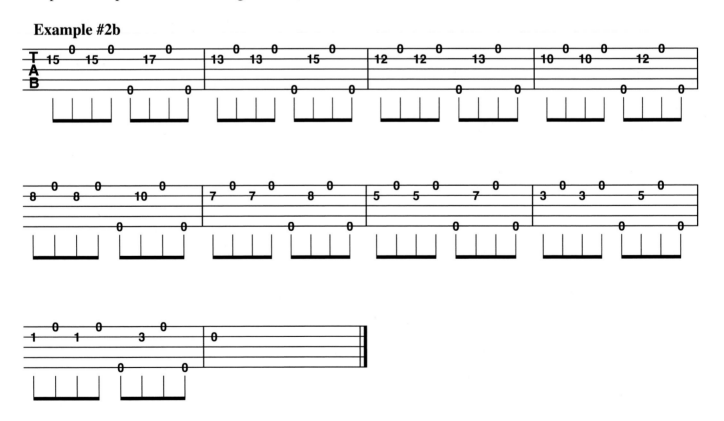

Use these two rolls to create your own melodies on the second string. Or, using your ear, find melodies to songs and try to fit them into these rolls.

Third String

The notes of the G scale are shown on the third string.

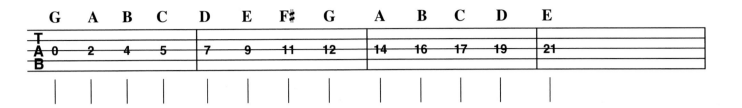

Use the same forward roll (Roll #1) that we used for the second string, and follow the example in #1a.

Roll #1 (Forward Roll)

Track 48

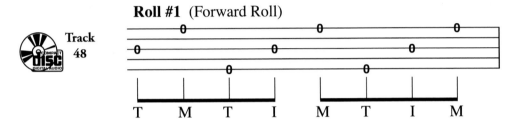

Example #1a

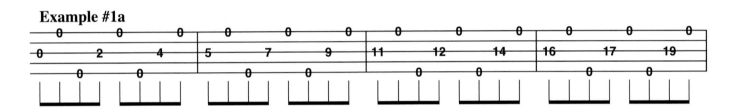

The Train 45 roll, also can be used, as in Example #2a.

Roll #2 (Train 45 roll)

Track 49

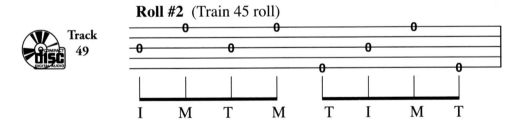

Example #2a

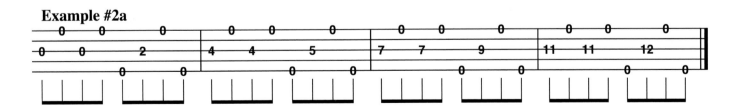

Since there are two strings above the third string we can use the forward/backward roll (Roll #3). Note that here the third string appears only twice, whereas it appears three times in the previous roll. Additionally, since four strings are sounded in the roll rather than three (as in both the forward roll and the Train 45 roll), more notes of the chord may be sounded. Practice Example #3a.

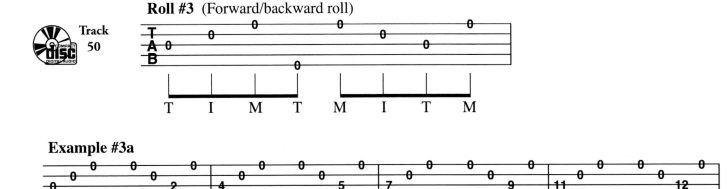

Another roll that works well is the alternating roll (Roll #4). As it's used here, the third string is played twice, with the melody on beats 1 and 3, as in Example #4a.

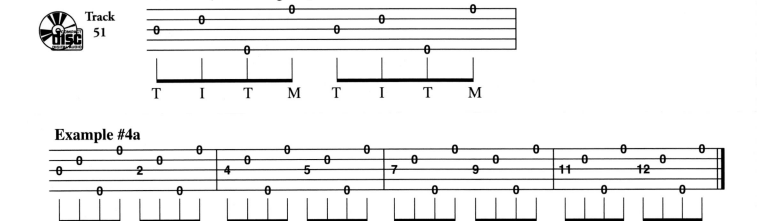

With the change shown in Roll #5, we can play a melody note on all the downbeats of the measure, as in Example #5a. This is an alternating roll.

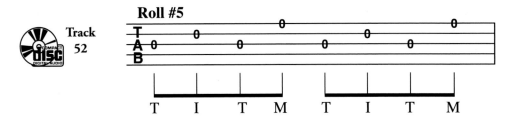

Example #5a

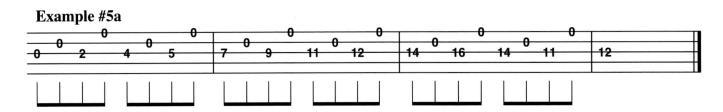

Fourth String

The notes of the G scale are shown on the fourth string.

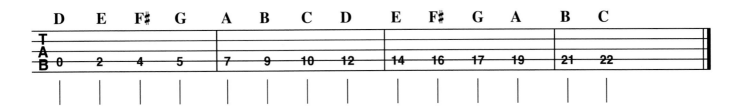

Roll #1 is a new configuration. Note that the fourth string appears three times. The rhythmical sound of this roll resembles that of the "Train 45" roll. You may notice that in choosing rolls for playing melodies on the fourth string, I don't show a roll where the index finger of the right-hand picks a note on the fourth string. I have a bias against using the index finger on the fourth string. I'll use it when I play in a single-string style, but not in a roll.

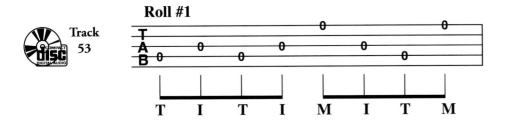

Example #1a is the G scale on the fourth string using this roll

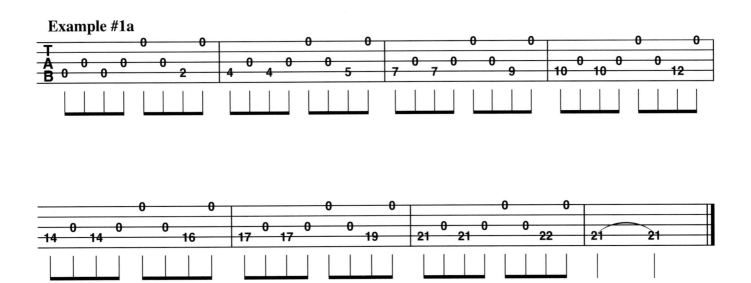

Roll #2 is a forward roll that doesn't use the fifth string, and as a result, it presents the melody in a rhythm similar to that in the forward rolls for the first and second string. Note that the fourth string appears three times, making it available for melody notes in those spots.

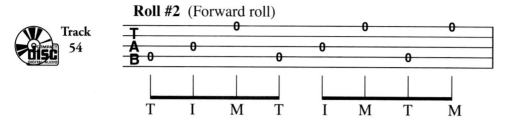

Roll #2 (Forward roll)

T   I   M   T   I   M   T   M

This rhythmical similarity will be evident when you practice example #2a.

Example #2a

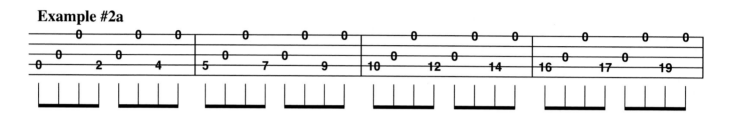

Roll #3 is a forward/backward roll, with the fourth string appearing twice (as when we used this roll on the third string).

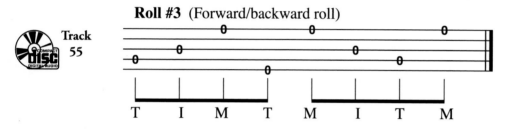

Roll #3 (Forward/backward roll)

T   I   M   T   M   I   T   M

Practice Example #3a.

Example #3a

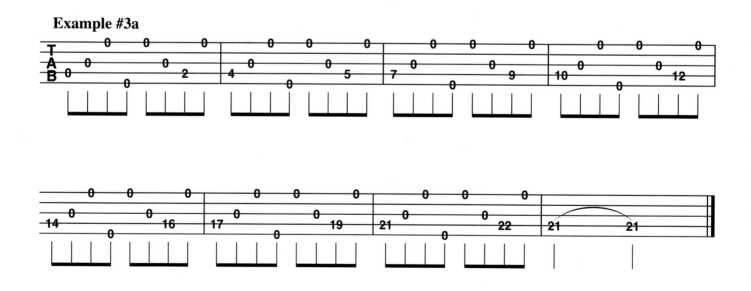

Roll #4 is the alternating roll.

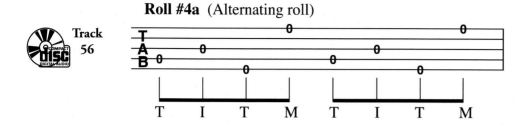

Example #4a is the alternating roll with scale tones.

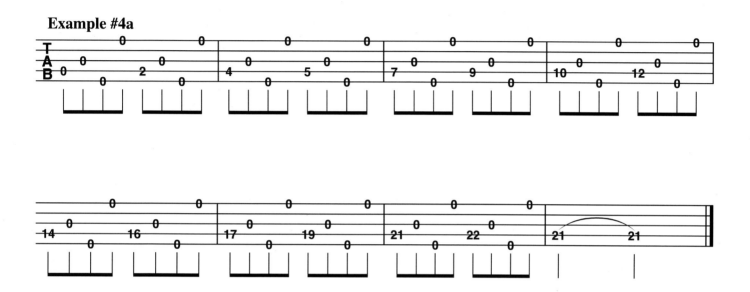

Roll #5 is a variation on the alternating roll. It omits the fifth string and puts a scale note on all the downbeats of the measure.

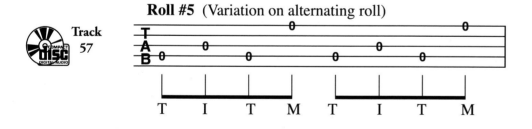

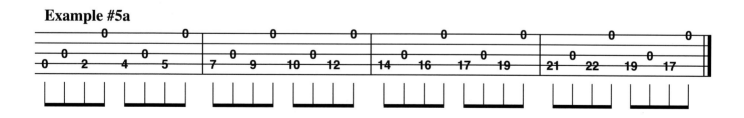

Working carefully and thoroughly through the material presented here will give you many of the mechanics needed to perform in a bluegrass banjo way.

Bury Me Beneath the Willow

To conclude this section we will work through the song "Bury Me Beneath the Willow" in several versions. Each version will present the melody on a different string or on a different set of strings.

Version #1

We will begin with the melody appearing entirely on the first string. You will notice that I have added the appropriate harmony note on the second string to follow the chord changes. If you are not familiar with the melody, play just the notes that appear on the first string and you will have the melody. The roll used is Roll #1, a forward roll, presented in the First String portion of this section.

Just a note that there are many ways to arrange this melody for the bluegrass banjo. The ones offered demonstrate the concepts that are presented in this section.

Track 58

Version #1 (Using forward roll, melody on 1st string)

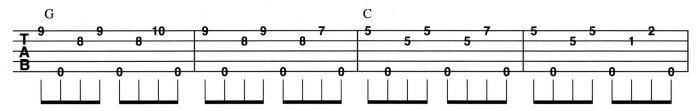

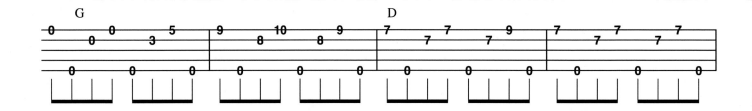

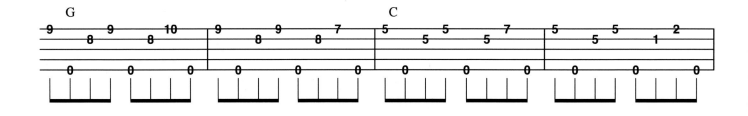

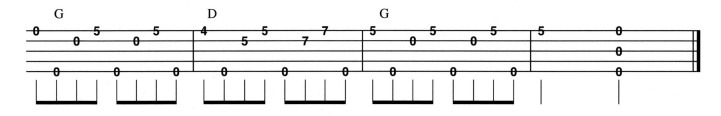

60

Version #2

This version will feature the same melody played on the second string. As in Version #1, I have added the harmony note on the first string, although you could play the first string open if you wish. It would not be a totally uncommon thing to do in bluegrass banjo playing. The roll used is Roll #1 from the Second String portion of this section.

Track 59

Version #2 (Using forward roll, melody on 2nd string)

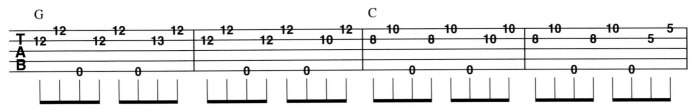

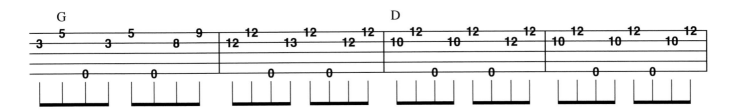

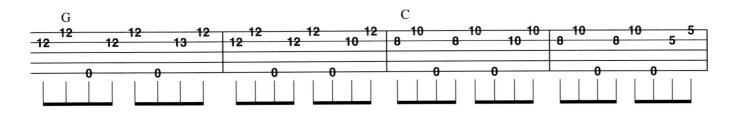

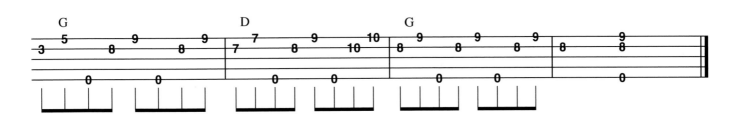

Version #3

Here the melody is lowered an octave. With this move we will need to use both the third and fourth string to accommodate the melody. Again, harmony notes are added. The forward/backward roll is used extensively with a forward roll used in measure six and again in measure fourteen.

Track 60

Version #3 (Using forward/backward roll and forward roll, melody on 3rd and 4th strings)

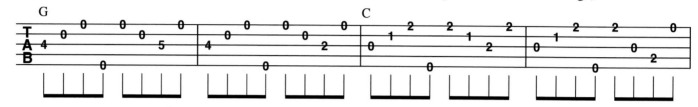

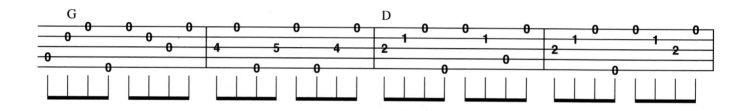

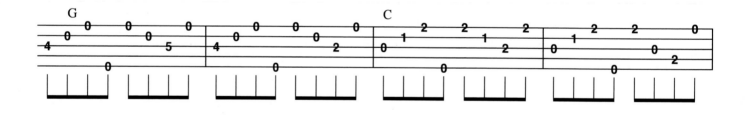

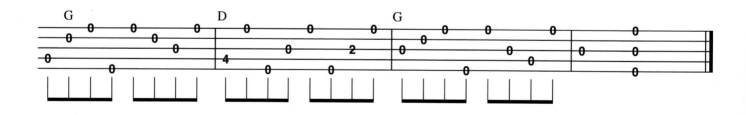

Version #4

Here the melody is presented on the fourth string. This is somewhat awkward and would not be normally done as shown here, but is presented as an exercise. As with the previous version the forward/backward roll is used in addition to the alternating pattern in measure six and fourteen.

Practice all the versions until you are comfortable with the use of the different rolls and string combinations. Also, listen to the differences in having the melody note as the highest note of the harmonic structure as in Version #1; or the same melody with one harmony note on one string above the melody, as in Version #2; or with the melody with two harmony notes above the melody as in Versions #3 and #4. The attention to those detailed choices of sounds can make playing more fun and interesting.

Track 61

Version #4 (Using forward/backward roll and alternating roll, melody on 4th string)

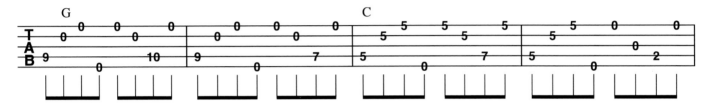

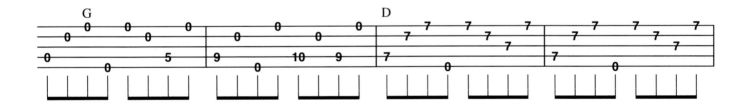

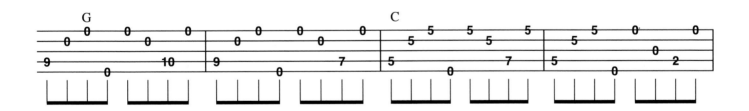

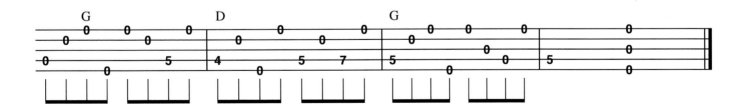

SECTION 4: Tools and Techniques

Up until now, the bulk of what we have covered has dealt with the right-hand picking patterns and usage. Now we will focus on left-hand technique. For the most part, the examples and exercises will not only offer technique challenges, but will also demonstrate musical concepts that can be put to use in developing your own arrangements.

Commonly Used Intervals

A chord is three notes that sound good together. Two notes that are played together are described by their distance from each other in the scale. That distance is referred to as an interval. The two most commonly played intervals are the interval of a third and the interval of a sixth. These intervals are what can be referred to as harmony notes i.e., notes that sound good together. Many times when two singers sing harmony, they are singing the intervals of a third or a sixth. There are other intervals that also sound good but this is what we are dealing with now.

Again, we will be using the notes of the G scale for all of the examples and exercises. The notes of the G scale, in order, are:

G A B C D E F♯ G

If we were to play a G note, the interval, or harmony, of a third above would be the B note. If we were to play an A note, the interval, or harmony, of a third above would be the C note. If you followed with this template up the scale, you would have the scale harmonized in thirds. Also, G can be viewed as the third below the B note.

If we were to play the B note, the interval, or harmony, of a sixth would be the G note above the B. Again, the B note can be viewed as a sixth below the G. If we followed this pattern up the scale, we would have a scale harmonized in sixths. These concepts will become clearer as you play through the examples and exercises.

Thirds on the First and Second Strings

Example #1 begins with the second string, B, and the harmony note of a third, D, on the first string. From there the pattern continues with the notes of the G scale found on the second string, and the harmony of a third on the first string. To reiterate, these may also be thought of in reverse, in that the D note is a third above the B, but the B is also a third below the D. You will notice that these positions will look like parts of chord forms that we have used in previous sections.

The technique component of this example is the left-hand fingering that is indicated. There are several ways to finger these intervals but the way suggested is one that offers a great deal of flexibility. It is used by many players and creates a smooth, efficient, disciplined fingering method. Note that there are only two positions in the whole of Example #1: when the notes are on the same fret, the third finger frets the first string and the second finger the second string; when the notes are one fret apart, the third finger is on the first string, the first finger on the second string.

Track
62

Example #1: 1st and 2nd String (third)

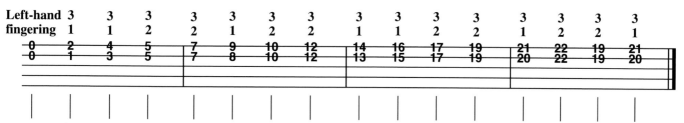

Guide Finger

In each example and exercise, one finger will be shown to fret all the notes on a certain string. The one finger that frets all the notes on a string becomes a guide finger and helps you find your way up and down the neck. In Example #1, the third finger frets all the notes on the first string. In Example #2, the fourth finger frets all the notes on the first string. In Example #3, the second finger frets all the notes on the third string. In Example #4, the second finger frets all the notes on the fourth string. And in Example #5, the third finger frets all the notes on the fourth string.

The exercise below couples the positions learned in Example #1 with the alternating pattern of M I M T. After you have played through the exercise, try other rolls and positions in different combinations until you feel comfortable with all the shifts and the sounds of the different rolls.

Exercise #1

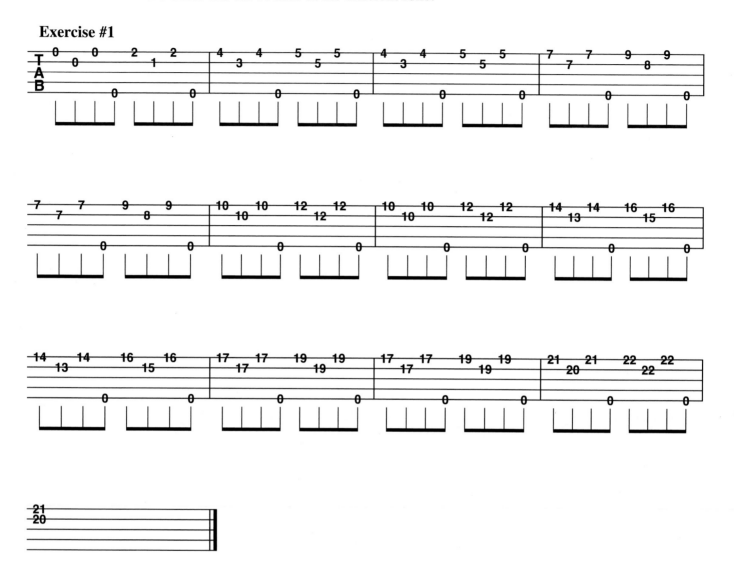

Sixths on the First and Third Strings

Example #2 begins on the third string fretted at the fourth fret and the first string fretted at the fifth fret, creating the interval of a sixth, i.e., B to G. The example continues up the notes of a G scale as far as possible. Again, the fingering is shown and should be followed: all the notes on the first string are fretted with the fourth finger, and the notes on the third string are fretted with the second or first finger. Again, there are only two positions in the whole of this exercise: one where the two fingered notes are one fret apart, and one where the fingered notes are two frets apart.

Track 63

Example #2: 1st and 3rd String (sixths)

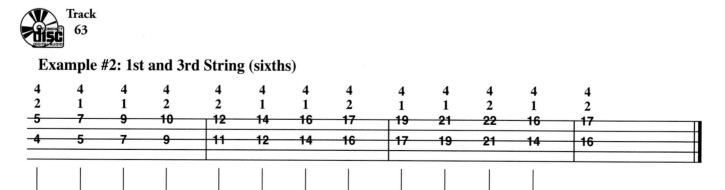

66

This exercise pairs the position of a sixth on the first and third strings with a forward roll. Again, after you become comfortable with all the maneuvers, try other rolls and combinations of position moves.

Example #2

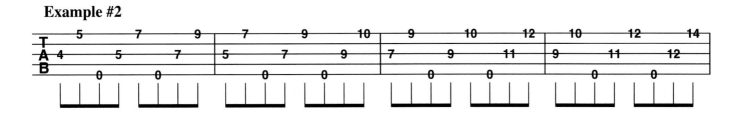

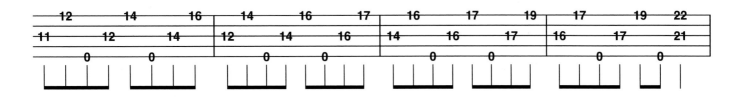

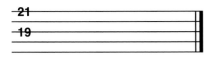

Thirds on the Second and Third Strings

Example #3 begins on the G note of the open third string, with the third above the B note on the open second string. Here the two positions are either one fret apart or on the same fret. Again, pay close attention to the fingering shown, as the second finger frets all the notes played on the third string.

Track 64

Example #3: 2nd and 3rd String (thirds)

The exercise below, in thirds on the third and second strings, features a forward/backward roll. Be sure to get the fingering correct and, as with all exercises, try different combinations of rolls and orders of positions. Create your own exercises.

Exercise #3

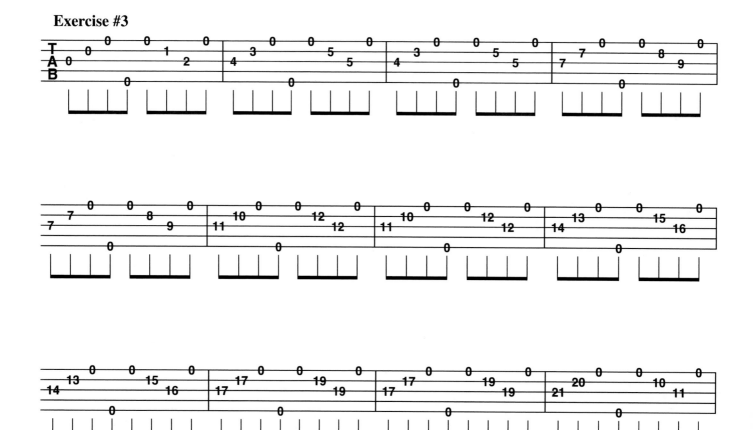

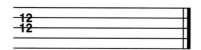

Sixths on the Second and Fourth Strings

Here we combine notes on the fourth and second strings to create the interval of a sixth. In this example, the second finger frets all the notes on the fourth string and acts as the guide finger.

Track 65

Example #4: 2nd and 4th String (sixths)

1	1	3	3	1	3	3	1	1	3	3	1	3	3	1
2	2	2	2	2	2	2	2	2	2	2	2	2	2	2

```
-0----1----3----5----|--7----8----10---12---|--13---15---17---19---|--20---22---19---20--||
-0----2----4----5----|--7----9----10---12---|--14---16---17---19---|--21---22---19---21--||
```

Exercise #4 adds some variety to this group of exercises, using the alternating pattern.

Exercise #4

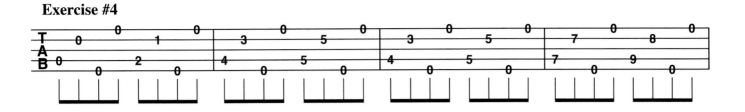

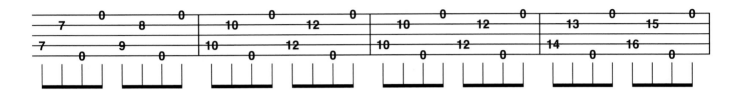

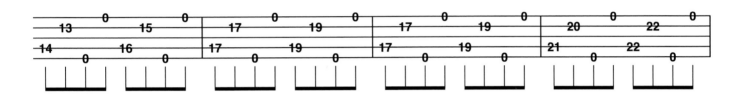

Thirds on the Third and Fourth Strings

Notes on the fourth and third strings are used to express the interval of a third. Start on an E note on the fourth string (to start on the open D note we need to be able to play the interval of third, F♯, which is the fourth string at the fourth fret. We can't fret two notes on the same string and have them sound at the same time).

Track
66

Example #5: 3rd and 4th string (thirds)

0	1	2	1	1	2	2	1	1	2	1	1	2	1	1
2	3	3	3	3	3	3	3	3	3	3	3	3	3	3

```
|--0---2---4---5----|--7---9---11--12---|--14--16--17--19---|--21--17--19-----||
|--2---4---5---7----|--9---10--12--14---|--16--17--19--21---|--22--19--21-----||
```

For Exercise #5, we are using a roll that is I T I M I T I M. In this exercise, the third finger on the fourth string is the guide finger.

Example #5

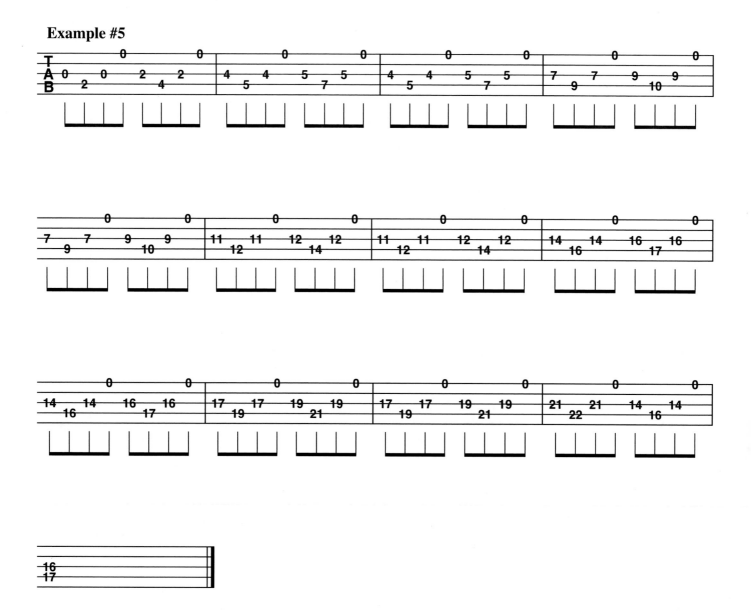

Practice the above examples and exercises to gain a facility in maneuvering through the left-hand fingerings of the many positions required to play the intervals of the third and sixth. Experiment with different rolls than those shown and skip between the different sets to gain insight into their use and sound. Develop your ear to hear these intervals and watch other players as they use them.

Using Thirds and Sixths

One use of the intervals of a third and a sixth is that it quickly harmonizes a melody. The first eight bars of the melody for the great old standard "Grandfather's Clock" is harmonized in several versions demonstrated below.

Version #1 has the melody on the first string harmonized by using the intervals of a sixth below on the third string.

Track 67

Version #1

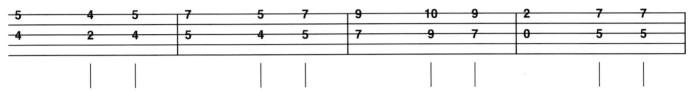

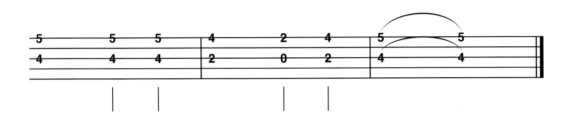

Version #2 has the melody on the second string harmonized by using the intervals of a third above on the first string.

Track 68

Version #2

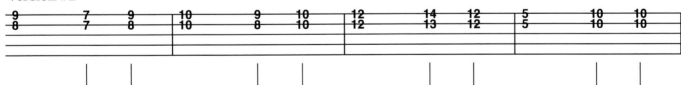

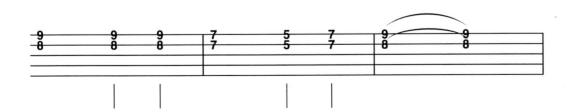

71

Version #3 has the melody on the second string as in Version #2, but with the melody harmonized below in sixths on the fourth string. This will give the same results as Version #1, but now on different strings. It is very useful to know how to get the same notes in different places.

 Track 69

Version #3

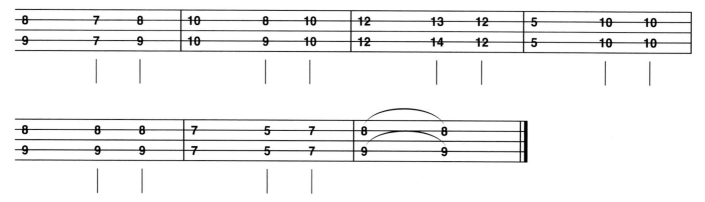

Version #4 has most of the melody on the third string with the lowest melody notes on the fourth string. The harmony of thirds is on the second string for most of the melody and on the third string for the lowest melody notes.

 Track 70

Version #4

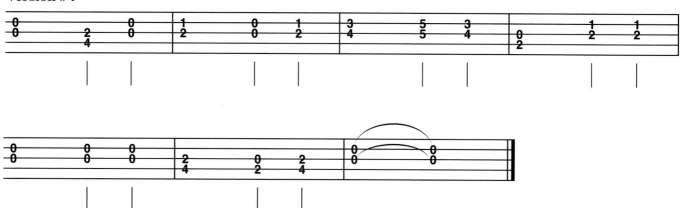

Version #5 has the melody on the fourth string, with the harmony of thirds on the third string.

 Track 71

Version #5

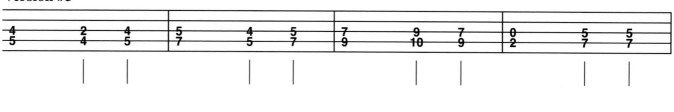

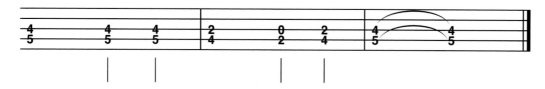

There are times when this system does not work as neatly as I have shown. For instance, if we wanted to have the melody on the second string and harmonize the third below on the third string, we would encounter some harmony notes that do not fit the chord of the song at that moment. At that point the harmony note needs to be adjusted up or down to match a note of the chord. The common solution on those occasions is to play the harmony of a fourth (in these cases, the fourth below). The numbers in parentheses are the harmonies of a third. In the first measure of Version #6 below, the harmony of a third below would be an E note. The E note in a G chord is not wrong, and in fact will sound good, but the note of the chord we want, that is part of the G triad, is a D note a fourth below. In the fourth measure, the harmony of a third for the melody note of A is an F♯. F♯ does not fit the triad of a C chord, the harmony of that measure. To adjust for this we go down a fourth to an E note, which is part of the C chord. Sounds complicated, but with time it will become clear. This is a time to develop your ear to quickly identify those errant sounds and replace them with chord tones.

Track
72

Version #6

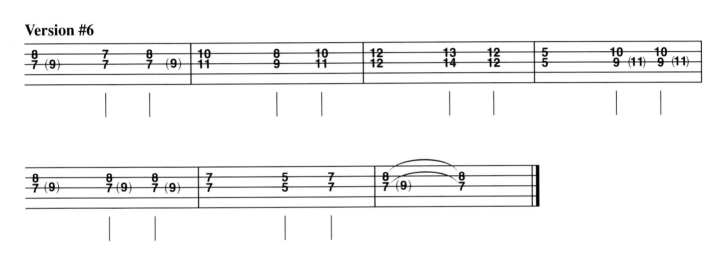

73

Scales and Arpeggios

There are many forms of scales, and knowledge of them is critical. In the Roll Logic section we viewed them in the key of G on one string at a time. The G-scale forms presented here are organized to be played across the strings in closed positions (no open strings). Since there are no open strings, each scale shape and arpeggio is movable to produce scales and arpeggios in all the keys. These should be learned for a full understanding of the fingerboard. Also developing the technique required to play these examples smoothly and efficiently will be a great boon to your playing. The left-hand fingering is shown. These scales and arpeggios also demonstrate a useful right-hand technique, often referred to as "single-string" playing.

Single-String Playing Technique

This technique resembles the flat-pick technique used by guitar and mandolin players. With a flat pick the two directions available are a downstroke and an upstroke of the pick. Additionally, several of the notes played in succession may be on the same string, and so we abandon the notion of playing in a roll pattern. For banjo players using finger picks, the technique is achieved with the thumb picking the downstroke and the index finger picking the upstroke. The logic that results in a smooth playable sound is that the thumb picks all the notes on the downbeat and the index finger picks the notes on the upbeat, as in Example #1.

Example #1

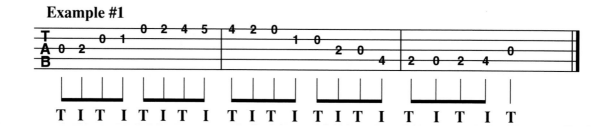

The same technique is used for the performance of the arpeggio, as in Example #2.

Example #2

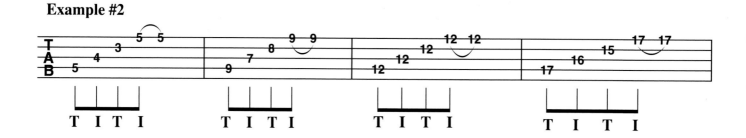

G Scales and Arpeggios

These are presented in a descending fashion, followed by an ascending arpeggio. The examples used come from a common ending in swing, western swing, and occasionally bluegrass music, and are a fun and instructive two measures. Note that there is an eighth note rest at the first of the two-measure phrases. There are many left-hand fingerings demonstrated here, so be sure to pay special attention to them.

The G scale and arpeggio in Example #1 begin on the tonic, or root, G note of the scale.

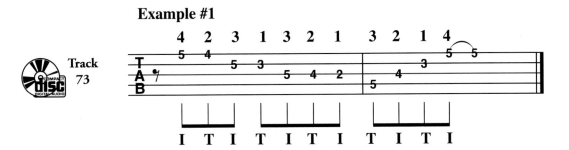

Example #2 also begins on the tonic, but has a different form and left-hand fingering.

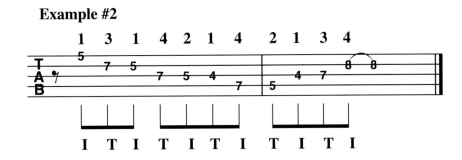

Example #3 also begins on the tonic and is yet another left-hand fingering.

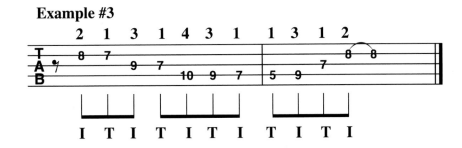

Example #4 begins on the third tone of the scale, B, and the arpeggio is the G chord from B to B.

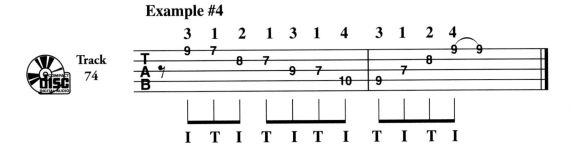

Example #5 also begins on a B note but has a different form and fingering. I suggest using the third finger as a barre (lay finger flat) to fret the notes on the first, second and third strings. Achieving a smooth transition will require extra practice. This barre technique is used frequently.

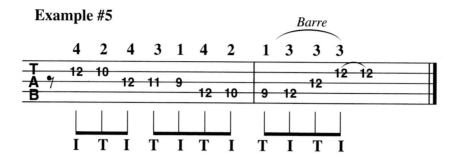

Example #5

Example #6 begins on the fifth tone of the scale, D, and the arpeggio again uses the third finger barre to fret the first through fourth strings.

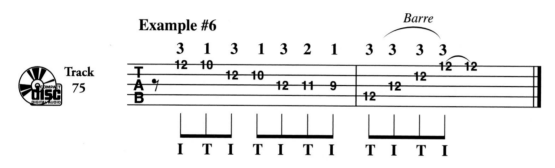

Example #6

Track 75

Example #7 also begins on the fifth tone of the scale and uses a first-finger barre to fret the strings.

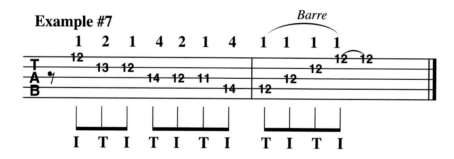

Example #7

Example #8 begins on the tonic note, now an octave above the scale and arpeggio in Example #1, but again offers a different fingering.

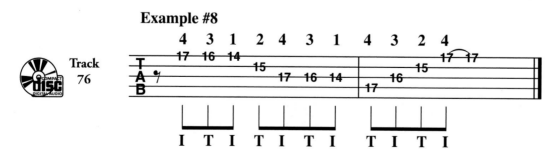

Example #8

Track 76

SECTION 5: Creating Solos to Songs

There is a strong tradition in bluegrass banjo of developing solos that express the melody of the song. These solos, also referred to as breaks, usually are not exact renderings of the melody, but are the bones of the melody surrounded by rhythmical and harmonic notes supplied by the rolls. Added to the arrangements are common bluegrass banjo ways of expressing melodic ideas through the use of the pull-off, hammer-on, and slide.

The tune presented here is the old standard American ballad "Jesse James." The song has been done in a bluegrass style by many performers. It contains common melodic and harmonic ideas found in numerous bluegrass songs and makes an excellent model for this exercise.

Jesse James

It is often said that music is like a language. In this exercise, the melody is the meaning we are trying to communicate. The bare bones melody is presented here. Play through it to get a good handle on the melody. Learning the melody of any song is the very first step in creating a solo. Also play through the chord changes as you hum the melody to yourself to get a sense of how the melody and chords fit together

Track 77

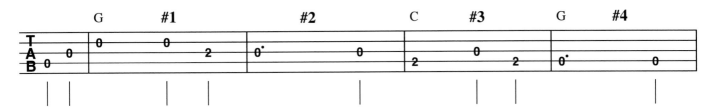

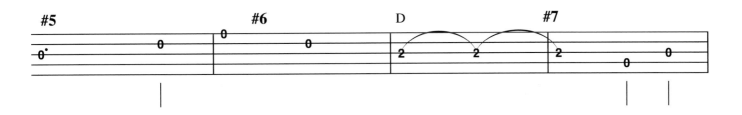

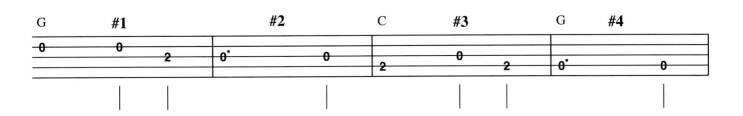

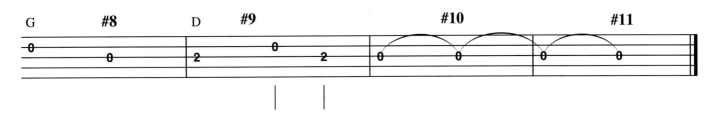

Musical Synonyms

Rather than think of the tune as a whole, I have divided the melody into eleven different musical phrases and numbered them accordingly above the measure. Below are corresponding phrases arranged in commonly performed bluegrass banjo style. Example #1a is one way that a bluegrass banjo player might express the melody of the first phrase. Other ways are given in Examples #1b through #1g. These variations may be thought of as musical and stylistic synonyms for the melodic meaning of the first phrase. Many of these banjo ideas have been covered in earlier sections. If the ideas are new, learn them now.

The choices presented may be viewed and learned as "licks," or rehearsed phrases, and performed as modules or motifs. It is helpful to think of them as how banjo players express melodies. The choices can and should be learned and rehearsed so that they come to your fingers as easily as words to your mouth. We do not write down and rehearse every conversation we have during a day, but draw upon a lifetime of language practice. The same can be true for music-making, but it takes a lot of practice and rehearsal to perform them so the music flows "trippingly" from the fingers.

The choices here become a part of the language of bluegrass banjo playing. There are many other words to learn but this is the beginning. Listen to other players for the synonyms, or "licks," if you like, that they use that are different. Try to get a sense of melody out of everything you hear and learn. What melody does this lick express? My mentor, Eddie Shelton, could sing the main focus of everything he played. Learn these lick-melodies and add them to your lexicon.

Each one-measure phrase below has a number of choices and always the "a" choice is straightforward and uses no slides, hammer-ons, or pull-offs. Also notice that the last note of each choice, indicated in parentheses, is the first note of the next melody phrase. As you play each choice, play the note in parentheses and it will help give you a sense of completion of the phrase.

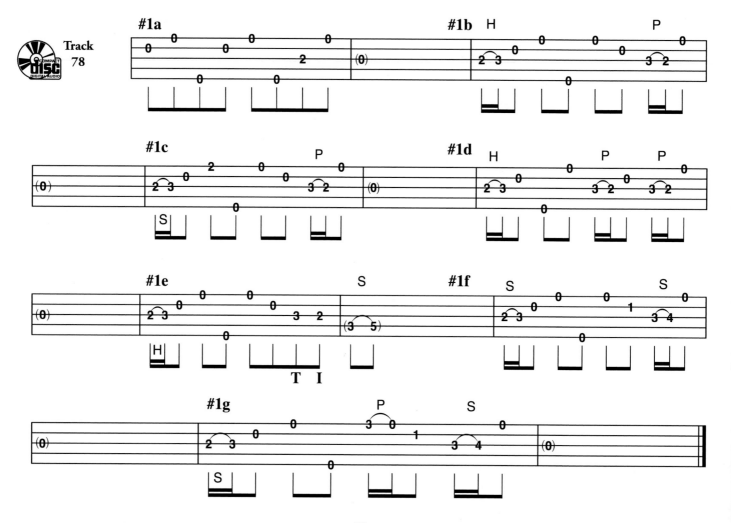

Track
79

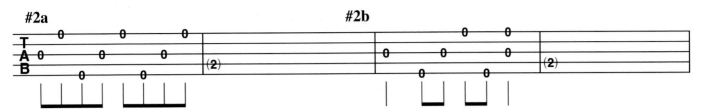

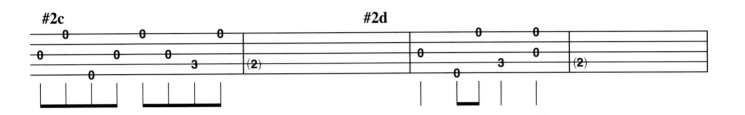

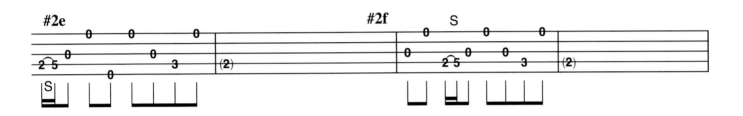

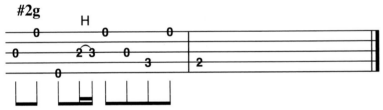

Track
80

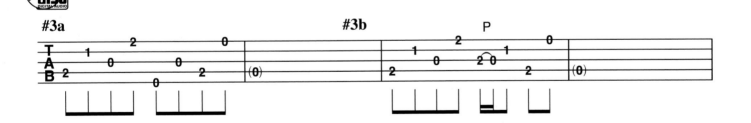

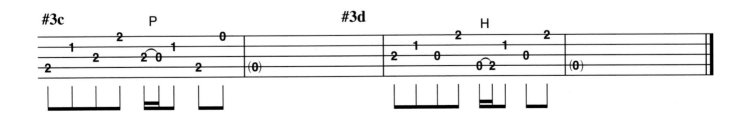

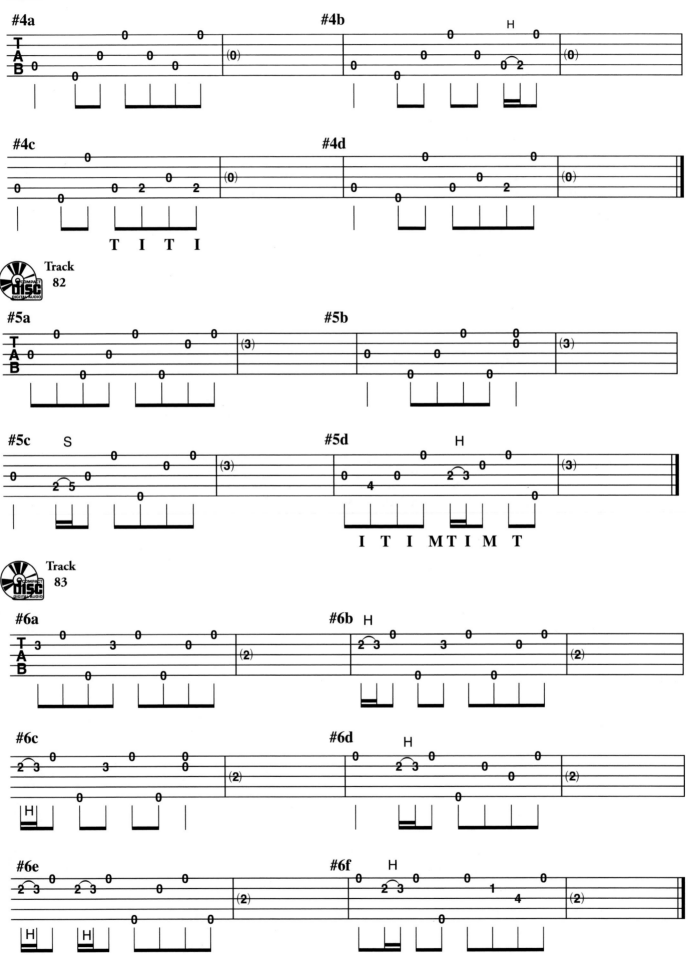

Note that the melody in Phrase #7 is two measures long and, vocally, is a held note. Bluegrass banjo players seem to use these two measures to feature an ear-catching roll, or the second measure to play pick-up notes leading back to the next melody phrase. A hint about bluegrass songs: when a song features the 5 chord (in this case D) in the middle of the chord pattern, the melody note is usually the second tone of the scale (in this case A). It happens a lot and should be noted. The Phrase #7 choices are important, as you will use them in many songs.

Track 84

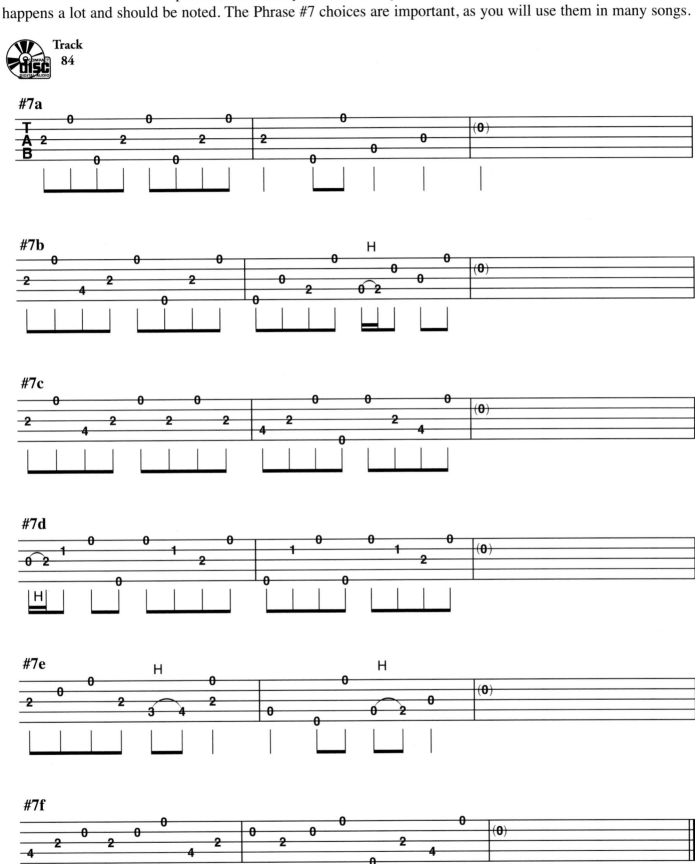

81

Track 85

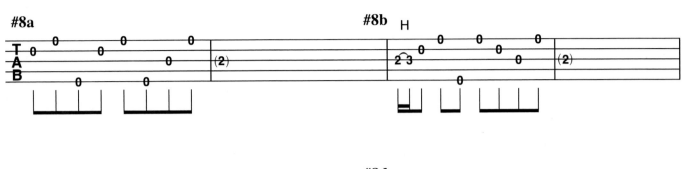

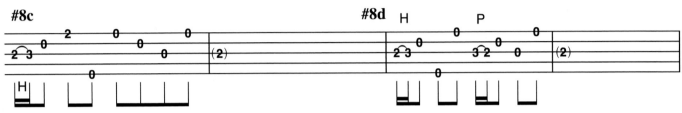

Track 86

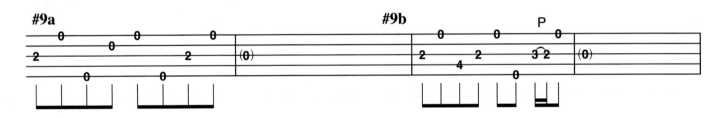

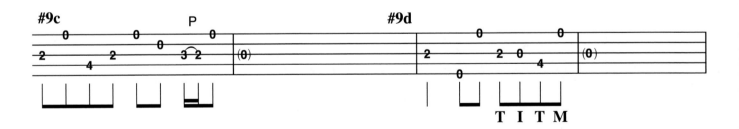

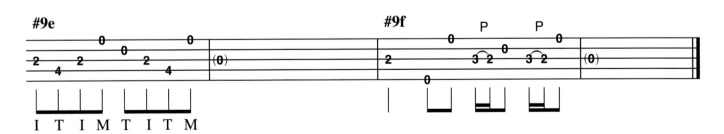

Phrase #10 is the last note of the melody, usually the tonic note, or G in our example. This is the spot where banjo players traditionally use the phrase I call "The Lick." The choices offer several variations. Phrase #11 is a measure of fill-in that can be used for pick-up notes leading back to the top. Here are several ways players fill this measure if not going back to the beginning.

Track
87

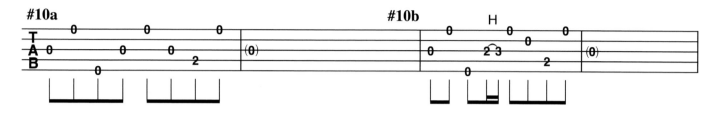

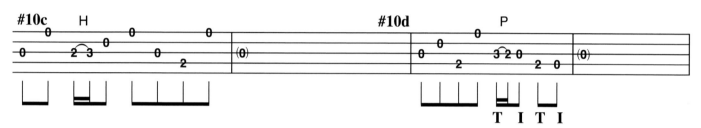

Track
88

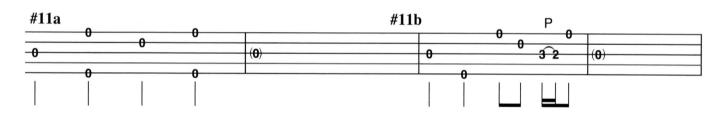

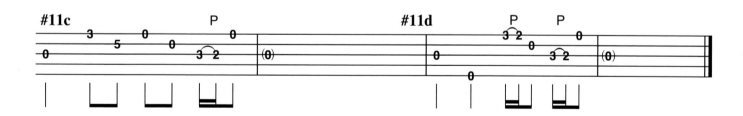

83

Jesse James Using all "A" Choices

One way to approach this material would be to learn the tune using all the "A" choices. After that, you could play the entire piece adding only one new choice at a time to get a sense of how this exercise feels. Keep practicing the piece until you feel comfortable making many choices. This whole process may take some time, but it is a method many players use: for each melody phrase find the best, cleverest, wittiest, most expressive way to perform the phrase in a bluegrass banjo style, then put all the phrases together to form the full arrangement.

Track 89

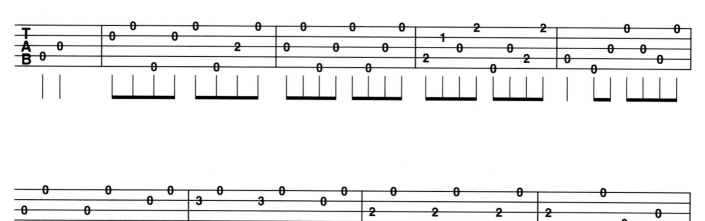

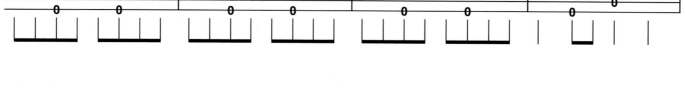

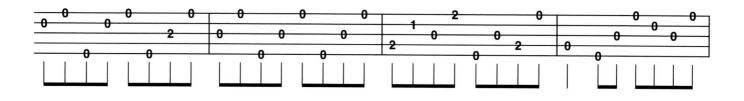

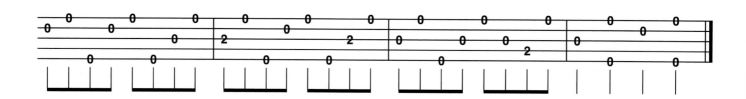

Jesse James Using Mixed Choices

This version offers only one of many, many of the arrangements that are possible by selecting from the many choices offered. I have indicated above each measure the number and letter choice I have made.

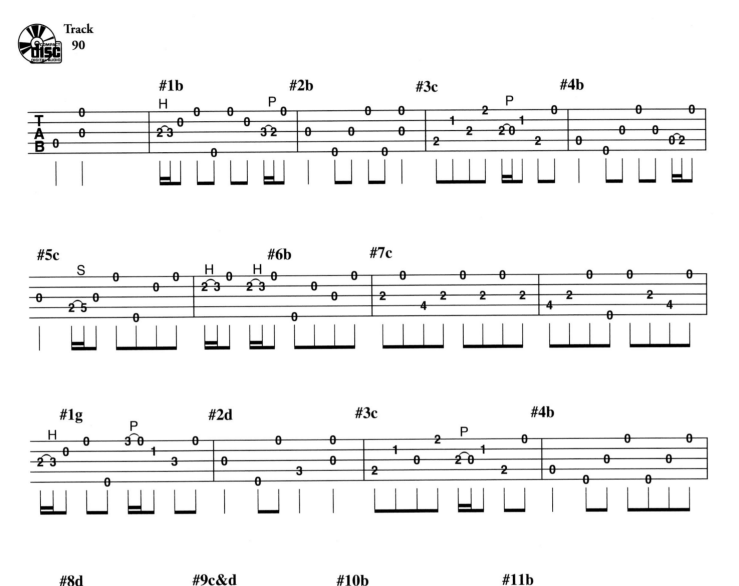

A Note on Improvising

The approach used above with "Jesse James" can lead to insights into improvising in the bluegrass banjo style. Often what sounds totally spontaneous is, in fact, many stylistic melodic modules, choices similar to the ones in "Jesse James," rehearsed and performed in an order decided in the moment by the player. After you have worked through the "Jesse James" choices and have them in your fingers, find other songs that have a similar chord progression or a similar melody, and try your hand at the art of improvising by making those choices on the fly. As my good friend Gerald Jones reminds students, "If you don't know the tune they are playing, play the one you do know that is closest to it."

SECTION 6: Songs

Now that you have worked through the sections, you can put all you have learned to use as you build a repertoire of standard bluegrass songs. The songs in this section have been selected and arranged to use many of the elements that have been presented in the earlier sections. Good picking

Track
91

Ground Hog

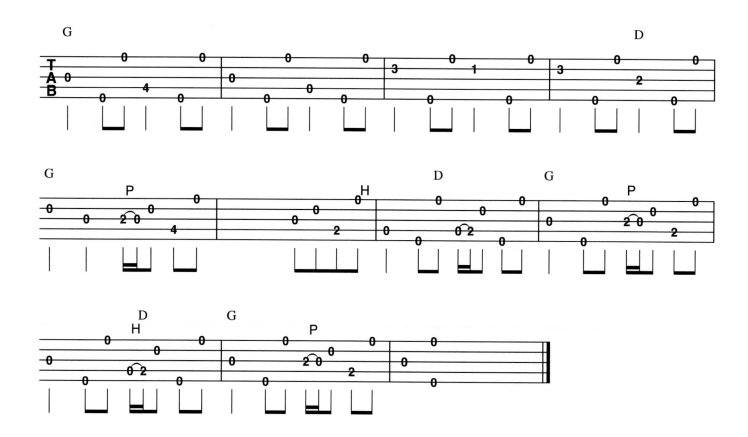

Wildwood Flower #1

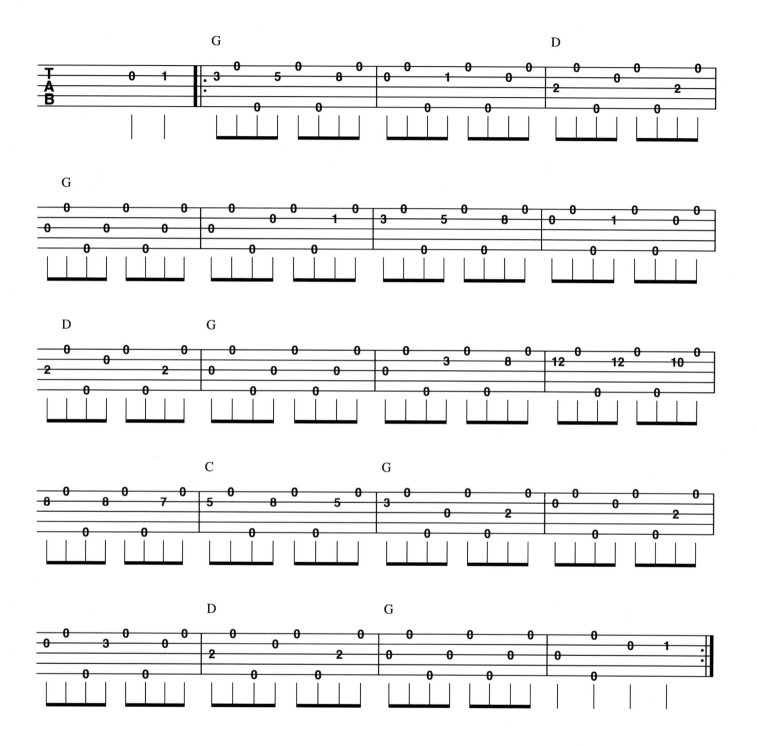

Wildwood Flower #2

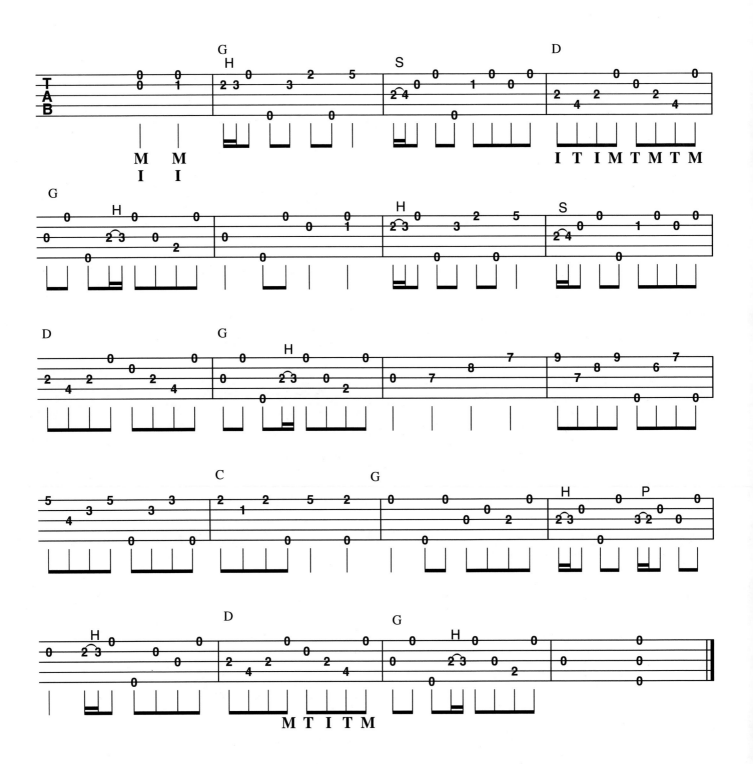

Track 94

Lost All My Money

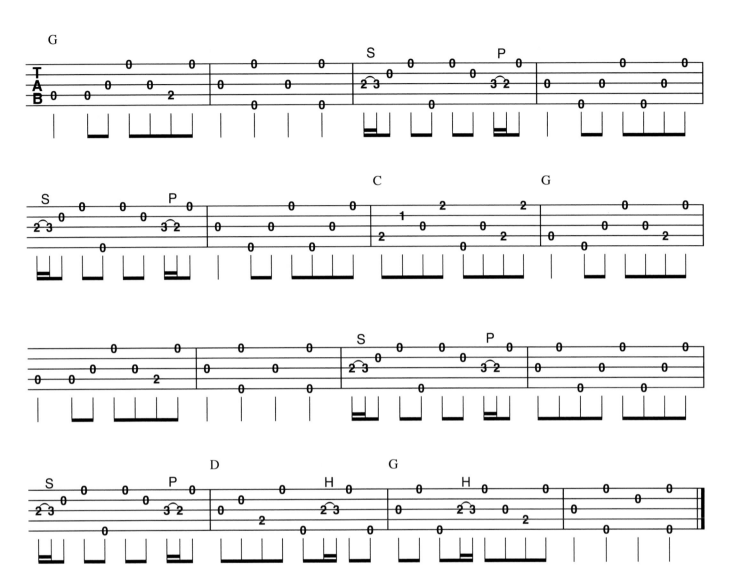

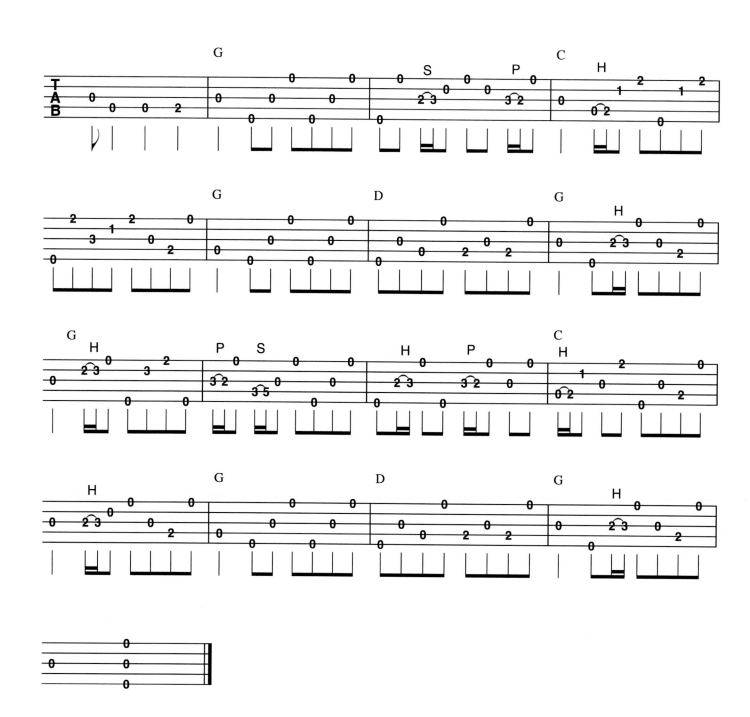

Nine Pound Hammer

Worried Man Blues

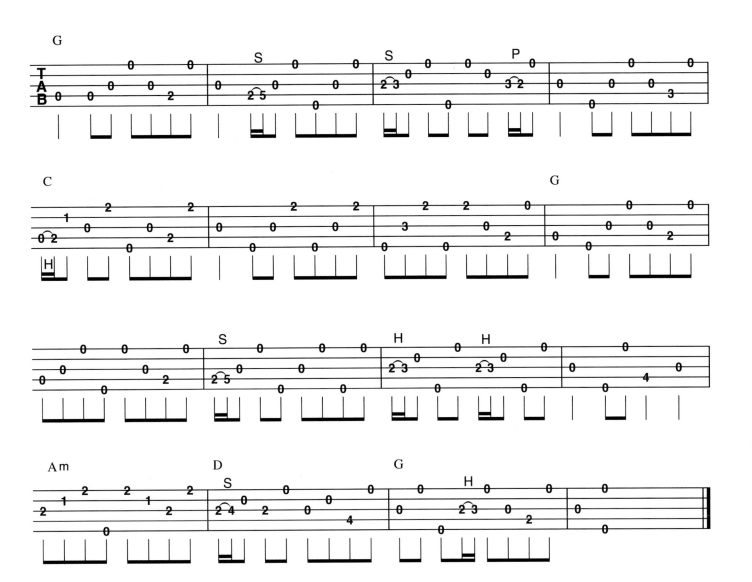

Train 45

Old Country Church

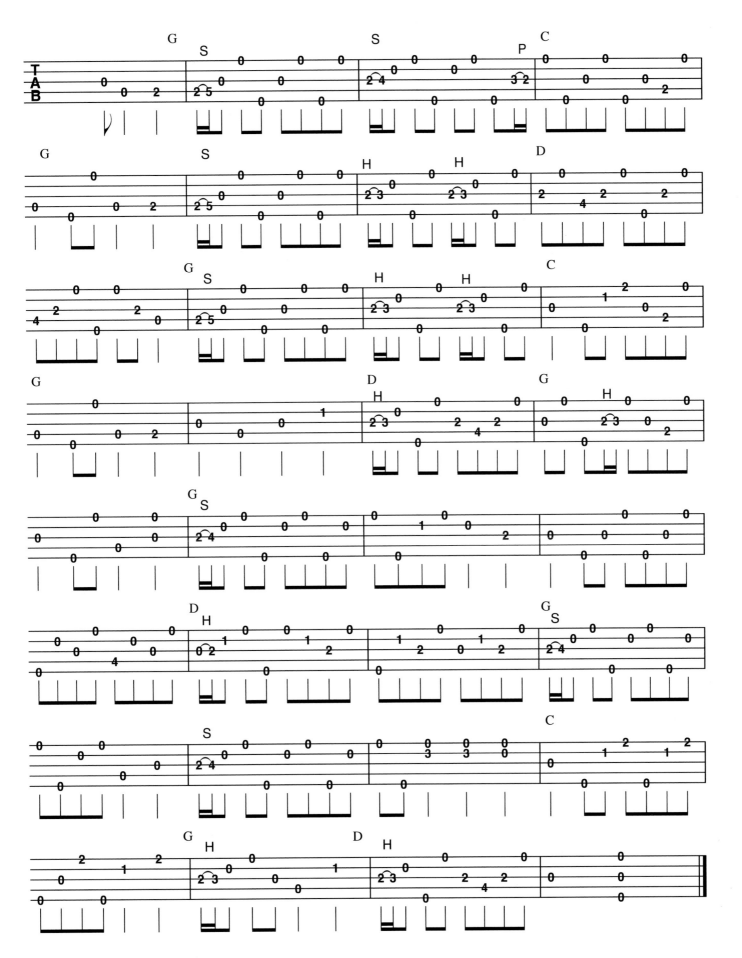

Kneel at the Cross

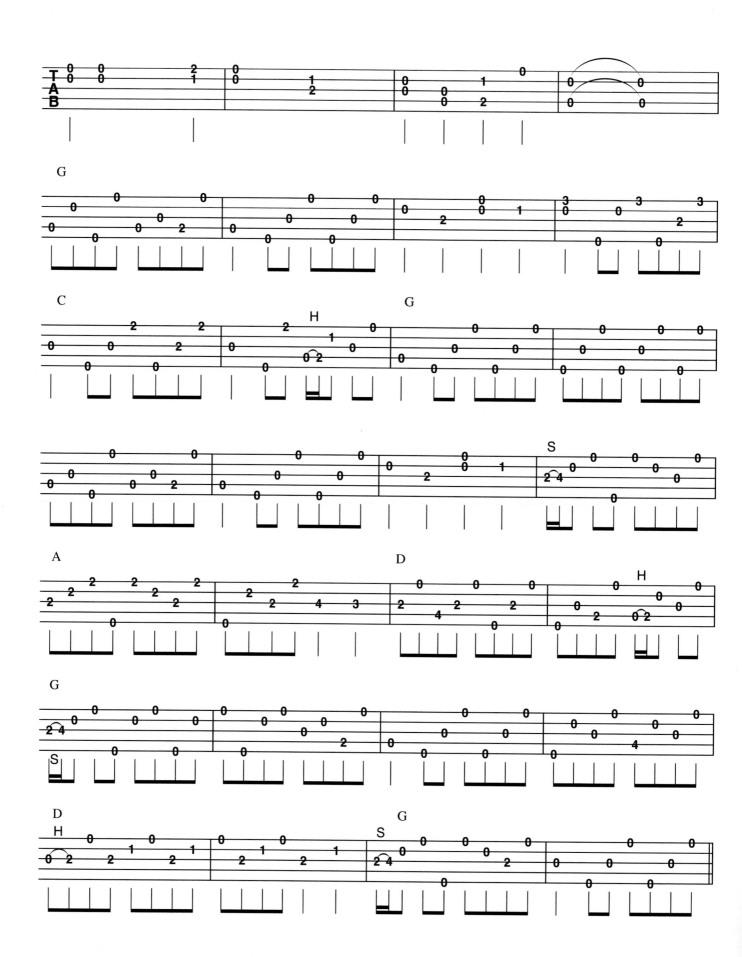

Kneel at the Cross (continued)

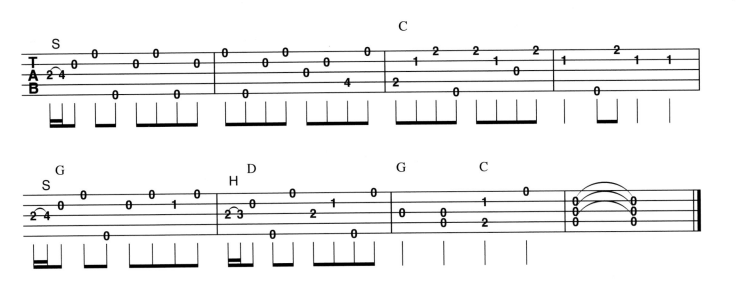

Alan Munde

Alan Munde needs no introduction to long-time Bluegrass fans. From his early creative work with Sam Bush in Poor Richard's Almanac to his traditional bluegrass apprenticeship with Jimmy Martin and the Sunny Mountain Boys to his 21-year stint anchoring the landmark Country Gazette, Alan has blazed a trail as one of the most innovative and influential banjo players of all time. Along the way, Alan also recorded and contributed to numerous instrumental recordings, including the 2001 IBMA Instrumental Album of the Year - "Knee Deep in Bluegrass." Alan has supplemented his recorded work with several instructional publications for the banjo, and, since 1986, Alan has taught Bluegrass and Country Music at South Plains College in Levelland, Texas, a program which has produced many professional musicians nationwide. In recent years, Alan has performed and recorded as a duo with his South Plains faculty colleague (and former Gazette-mate) Joe Carr. Alan's extensive body of recorded work, his instructional materials, and his work at South Plains (including the annual "Camp Bluegrass") has solidified his status as one of the true "gurus" of the 5-string. Alan leads his own group, The Alan Munde Gazette.

Special Thanks

Special Thanks to Beth Mead for too many hours spent in layout of the book, to Carolyn Hegeler and Kitty Ledbetter for their careful proofreading, and to Mike Stahlman for his thoughtful input.